SALUTATIONS

A Memoir

SALUTATIONS

A Memoir

Argie Ligeros

WHERE INK MARKS **YOUR EVOLUTION**

Published by MorphLit Press | morphlitpress.com
An imprint of Voicespan Studios | voicespanstudios.com
Los Angeles, California

Cover design by: Debbie O'Byrne
Interior design and layout in collaboration with Igniting Souls
Paperback ISBN: 979-8-9994189-3-7
Hardcover ISBN: 979-8-9994189-4-4
E-book ISBN: 979-8-9994189-5-1
Library of Congress Control Number: 2025916744

Available in paperback, hardcover, e-book, and audiobook.

This is a work of nonfiction.
Some names and identifying details may have been changed
to protect the privacy of individuals.

Printed in the United States of America
First edition: October 2025

For more books that evolve with you, visit: morphlitpress.com

For Demian

CONTENTS

Preface

I was twenty when I took my first yoga class. Upon finishing, a voice in my head said, *You must promise to do this for the rest of your life. Nobody can take this away from you.* At that point, much was already taken from me. I trusted what I heard, sealed the promise, and practiced yoga for over fifty years.

I regard yoga as the worthiest of all pursuits, one that yields the greatest gifts. It is a noble exchange that consistently and justly returns the invested effort. Yoga has elevated my life more than anyone or anything. It bestowed upon me the strength to navigate grief and disease with grace.

If we are living to discover who we are, yoga has been my roadmap, my flashlight, my tuning fork, my high-tech navigational system, my guide, and my beacon. In my most difficult moments, it has been my hug, the hand that strokes my head, the calming whisper, the phrases that console me. Yoga opened a clear communication channel, allowing me to access my inner voice.

A tenacious yoga practice—the sweaty, grueling, consistent repetition of practicing postures thousands of times—rewards the body with optimum functionality and the appearance and essence of youth. Yoga cleanses and perfects, fine-tuning every system of the body: endocrine, cardiovascular, nervous, muscular, mental, and structural systems . . . everything!

Five decades after I took my first yoga class, I repeat the postures, answering life's questions with clarity and forward movement, overcoming sadness, anger, and anxiety. I also do them for fun. My practice is my best friend to whom I turn for advice—the one true source of solace for me, a peace that resonates within my heart and soul.

I appreciate soothing words or advice offered by friends, but internal answers are genuine. Advice from another person is their viewpoint, expressed through their filter of reality. Yoga brings forth responses that become simple to act upon since they originate within you.

Yoga is an active meditation that establishes and reinforces the mind-body connection, opening up a dialogue between the two. It serves as a mirror that reflects and allows one to gaze within. What is seen enters the conscious mind, generating automatic awareness. It may be something physical. You might say, "Oh, I didn't realize my right hip is much tighter than my left," when sitting in a cross-legged position such as *padmasana*.

The mirror reveals something deeper: a samskara—an energy pattern. In Hindu thought, a samskara is a mental imprint, a memory etched within. It may arise from our family lineage, a pivotal life event, or a powerful influence. We all carry these imprints inside us. Most often, we are unaware of them, yet they quietly shape what we think and do. Through yoga and similar practices, we bring them to light. Once we see them, we can work through them. This helps us live in a way that feels truer and purer.

I've uncovered the stamps and impressions of my life. Doing so has allowed me to overcome difficulties—confront, transcend, alchemize, and use them to grow and evolve. It has also made me a teacher.

Instructing yoga has shown me that my unique ability is connecting people to the basics. Yoga is accessible to all. My role is to demystify it. I see myself as a normal person. I am not a yoga scholar. I've read some of the ancient texts, but not all. Occasionally, I eat meat. I enjoy a glass of wine at a dinner party.

Self-realization and enlightenment are my goals and the traditional aims of the practice, but yoga also enhances my mundane life, keeps me fit, grounded, and able to cope with adverse conditions. It makes me kinder, more compassionate, and happier. It heightens my awareness of the world I inhabit. My observations are keener, enabling me to synthesize why relationships and events arise and what I can learn from them.

When I started teaching in the late 1970s, yoga was unknown or viewed as somewhat bizarre. As a former competitive gymnast and avid athlete, I made the case for the practice of yoga to improve performance, lessen the risk of injury, and increase recovery rates. I didn't present it to activate the latent spiritual energy called *kundalini*. I didn't mention that the energy flows more freely through the *nadis*, or energy conduits, in the subtle body. If I had used industry jargon, the yoga studio would have been empty. In those days, most people were not prepared to hear about such things.

My work has been to introduce yoga to reluctant or skeptical audiences. Even when someone's only goal is to get more flexible hamstrings, the intelligent force of yogic energy emerges. I have seen my students' lives change in profound ways. Yoga awakens muted wisdom, bringing clarity about one's purpose and direction.

As an instructor, my primary role is to plant the seed of practice, especially for those hesitant to begin.

Whether you are a yoga enthusiast or have never stepped foot on a mat, I wrote this book to share how devotion—imperfect, persistent, and intimate—illuminates a path through life's darkest moments and reveals the quiet, enduring strength within.

Greetings from the Author

This book began in Vail, Colorado, on the evening of December 21st, 2020, during a winter solstice party my then-husband and I were hosting. People were eager to gather. Everyone had their own pandemic story they were keen to share. A friend told me she was writing her memoir. As she described her experience working with a writing coach, Lisa Steinmetz, whom she met online weekly, she stopped in the middle of a sentence.

"Argie, you should write your memoir!" she said.

"Yes! I would like to do that," I replied without hesitation.

The following week was my first online writing session with Lisa. She assured me writing is a wonderful experience. "If you commit a little time each day in a quiet space, preferably upon awakening, the divine writer within will help you fill the pages," she said.

I am used to woo-woo, but this sounded esoteric even to me. I did as she prescribed.

When I started writing, surprising memories of people from my life poured in. It felt as if a divine writer was sending them from deep within my mind. These memories took shape on the pages of my notebook.

I wrote about them in a stream of consciousness—without judging and without worrying about grammar or style. I was writing only for myself, a mix of therapy and pure fun. What joy it was to relive those moments.

Five years after I began writing, I moved to a different city, entered into a new romantic relationship, and continued crafting my memoir. It's been a stop-and-start process, a passion project I carried with me, mind and spirit, with varying degrees of prominence.

This book is a set of encounters or salutations. They shaped the chapters, which follow the yoga sequence called the Sun Salutation. The poses in this series connect to the form, movement, and breath of life, expressed through people, events, and experiences.

This book features the number twelve, which appears throughout our existence. Twelve is also the number of major gods of Olympus worshipped by the ancient Greeks (my family heritage). Twelve governs and structures our lives: twelve hours of day and night, twelve months in the year, and twelve houses in an astrological chart—symbolizing completeness.

For me, it also holds personal significance. Just before my twelfth birthday, I experienced an unspeakable tragedy that changed the trajectory of my life. From that point on, I became a different person.

I salute you, the reader, as we meet in these pages. Together, we share the stories, thoughts, and feelings that unfold here.

The Sun Salutation has several variations. I have adapted the most basic one. *Surya Namaskar* was developed in India thousands of years ago to pay homage to the sun, regarded as the life-giving force of the universe. In Sanskrit, *Surya* means sun, and *Namaskar* means greeting. Honoring the vital energy that nourishes, heals, and purifies every living thing on the planet is an ancient practice that acknowledges the sun's power over our entire existence.

Traditionally, one starts the day by facing the sun and performing a moving meditation, flowing the body through space, pausing momentarily in each posture, then gracefully transitioning on to the next. The breath guides the rhythm and pace, inhaling and exhaling with the movements. Twelve postures complete the sequence. Four of them repeat twice. The full round finishes upon returning to the first posture. We repeat the series as many times as desired.

I estimate I've practiced the Sun Salutation series in this form or a similar variation over 50,000 times. The drawings of the postures throughout the book are sketches I have given my clients since I started teaching. I turn to it when I'm lost and unhappy, inspired and joyful and invite my students to do the same. The Sun Salutation is my refuge, safe space, and true home. It feels appropriate to me to present my life through this perspective.

The word *salutation* has many meanings. It can be a handshake, a nod, or a toast. It can be a greeting that wishes good health. It can mark someone's arrival or departure with words like "hello," "good morning," or "goodbye."

Like the Sun Salutation, it can also be an act of honor or ceremony.

The pages of this book embrace the resonant layers of salutation, especially of the people from my past, greeting them once again. The act of saluting the sun is an act of reverence and respect. I honor and pay tribute to the unique collection of people who have helped shape my journey.

Within a metaphorical framework, I relate certain aspects and benefits of each posture to my personal life in each chapter. In the series of postures that comprise the Sun Salutation, you reach up with your gaze directed to the sky, dive and bow down to look behind, lift your head to peer forward, and stare within your body. I looked up into the heavens and asked God, angels, guides, or whoever—someone with special powers—to help me grieve. Other times, I have bowed to challenging, unexpected situations, drawing on my past for strength, guidance, and comfort.

When I strained to look onward and move forward amid tragedy, I sought answers within, delving into breathwork and meditation.

Along with the Sun Salutations postures, I have linked a chakra to each chapter. Chakra means "wheel" in Sanskrit. Ancient wisdom says we have three forms that work together in different spaces. The physical body, the astral body that holds our thoughts and feelings, and the causal body shows up as wisdom.

The chakras belong to the astral body. Yet they affect the mind, body, emotions, and spirit. They are like spinning centers that give and take energy. Chakras work best when they are in balance.

Today, many devices track our heart rate, sleep, calories, and energy use. But focusing on the chakras turns our attention inward. It helps us notice and understand the life force—chi or prana—that flows in us. I believe this focus adds depth to life. Western science is starting to study chakras. They are complex, but we can still grasp them in a simple way.

In my story, I use them in a personal and easy-to-follow style. Their colors and images show the bright, living parts of who we are—and they deserve our care.

After a yoga session, while relaxing on my back in the final posture known as *savasana* or dead man's pose, I've detected a whirring of energy in certain areas of my body—a heightened flow of energy.

When I feel deep joy or deep sadness, I sense it in my heart center, the Anahata Chakra. When I feel desire for someone, the Muladhara, or root chakra, comes alive.

I notice my emotions not only in my body, but also through the energy of the chakra system. This view adds another layer of meaning to my life.

I salute you and honor you for being here. I wish the light of the sun through the lens of yoga touches you while reading this book. May the energy and love of my heart chakra reach and expand your heart as you bend, bow, and plank through life and the pages ahead.

1. Roots

There are only two lasting bequests we can hope to give our children. One of these is roots, the other, wings.

—Johann Wolfgang von Goethe

Mountain Pose
Tadasana

Tada means mountain in Sanskrit. Asana means pose or posture. Standing in Tadasana marks the beginning of the Sun Salutation series. You ready yourself for what's next by placing your feet together, spreading your toes, and sensing the soles of your feet connect securely to the surface beneath you. The muscles of your legs contract, lifting the knees and hugging the bones of the legs. The pelvis remains in a neutral position, the spine straight, shoulders relaxed, and hands pressed together at the chest. You gaze ahead, fully focused. This posture fosters a sense of centeredness, connection, stability, and strength.

Earth Star Chakra
Vasundhara ~ Daughter of the Earth

The amber-brown Earth Star Chakra, the grounding point for the entire chakra system, provides a foundation, an anchor for physical and spiritual well-being. It governs a person's connection to their physical environment. Physical activity is one of the key ways to activate it, allowing the chakra to become vibrant and expansive. It is located in a person's energy field approximately twelve to thirty inches below the feet.

My Heritage

On May 16, 1954, at 9:34 p.m., I took my first breath in the Boulder Community Hospital. This was the closest hospital to residents of Lafayette, where my parents, aunt, uncle, and grandparents lived. Our little neighborhood had streets with names like Acropolis and Aegean Drive, Hercules Circle, and Titan Place. The Greeks who had immigrated and settled in Lafayette escaped the violent Turkish occupation to provide their children with a college education and a more prosperous life.

With their meager belongings, the Greeks who came before me from Chania, Crete, a charming port city, crossed the Atlantic. At the Ellis Island screening port, my grandparents arrived, and their last name, Ligerakis, changed to Ligeros. With enough money to purchase railroad tickets for themselves and their three small children, they headed west on a train and got off in Casper, Wyoming.

After they heard about laboring work, the Greek immigrants went to the nearby coal mines. I can't imagine a more horrific job. A coal miner's day involved going down a shaft into a bleak cave to mine black coal while inhaling silica and toxic air, and then, after hours of labor, emerging covered in black soot. They must have questioned and shed remorseful tears over their plan to flee the brutal Turkish occupation of Crete. The impact was apparent in observing my grandmother and grandfather.

My grandfather, παππούς, never spoke of his feelings concerning departure from Greece or starting over in a foreign land. His name was George or Γιοργος. From early morning to evening, he worked in the coal mines to give my dad and his siblings a better life than he had. He didn't speak much. I understand his silence to be his way of shutting off from pain. In doing so, he seemed devoid of joy. When he was home, he only moved when necessary—to address his bodily needs, scratch an itch, open his mouth to eat his meal, or get up to go to the bathroom. From the corner of the living room, he watched us grandchildren play, sitting in his stuffed armchair with no expression.

My grandmother, γιαγιά, bore the name Αργρρω (Argyros). My parents named me after her, following the tradition of naming the first female grandchild after her father's mother. She cooked and cared for everyone. I loved her so much. She cupped my face in her hands, looked at me with happy tears welling up in her eyes, and said, "καροτο, καρότο," (my heart, my heart). Her sacrifices gave her children and grandchildren the possibility of a better future in the United States. When she held my face in her hands, I knew that the struggles of first-generation immigration and leaving the life she knew were worth it for her. Despite the horrors of the Turkish occupation, she left behind the clear blue-green waters of the Aegean and the familiar environmental fragrances like wild thyme that permeate the island of Crete. Cooking was her pastime; she recreated the familiar aromas of Cretan dishes.

Grandpa George, a poor immigrant miner, endured the harsh winters and grueling conditions of Wyoming, Utah, and Colorado, which tested his resilience, but tragedy struck beyond the coal mines. He and Grandma lost their oldest son, Βασίλης (William). He died at twelve when a car hit him while he was riding his bicycle. My grandparents had four more boys. My father was the youngest. They named him Βασίλης (William), the same name as their deceased first son.

Dad, William (Billy)

Dad often said, "Argie, you can do anything if you put your mind to it." I remember watching the Miss USA beauty pageant with him on the little black-and-white TV screen. "Do you want to be Miss America someday? If that's something you might like to do, I know you can do it." I believed him. *Maybe I will become Miss America*, I thought.

My dad was my world—charismatic, successful, and driven. People I encountered later in my life, all of whom knew him, commented on his determination and drive. He wasn't tall but stood out with his slim, muscular body and black shock of hair that fell out of place and brushed across his forehead. He let me pluck his eyebrows. I can recall every inch of his face—chiseled jaw and straight, white teeth.

Dad paraded me around, introducing me to everyone. "You look like your father," they said. Everyone who heard this nodded in agreement, a response that made Dad radiate.

He was gone for long periods of time, driving transport trucks along with his brother Mike. Fueled by their parents' sacrifices, they pursued the American dream and excelled. Eventually, the driving led them to open Thermo King trucking franchises. Dad and Mike both became some of their top salesmen.

Dad accomplished so much at an early age. At 36, he owned two Thermo King franchises, was president of the Holy Trinity Greek

Orthodox Church, a 32nd-degree Mason, a pilot, and an accomplished golfer. He even had a trophy for the best-dressed man in Salt Lake City.

My Mother, Wanda

My mother's eyes never went unnoticed. People described them as Elizabeth Taylor eyes, bright, light, lavender-blue. Her black hair, which was teased at the crown to give her height, framed them. She usually styled her hair in a lacquered, smooth, elegant chignon and used bobby pins to hold every strand in place.

Mom smoked menthol cigarettes, even while driving with my sister and me in the car. She drew them from her gold synthetic leather case and lit them with her matching gold metal flip-top lighter. She took a big inhale as she snapped the lighter shut. It must have made her feel older and sophisticated. She was only 15 when I was born. "Five Foot Two, Eyes of Blue": She said that was her song because that's what she was. She loved music and played Dean Martin and Frank Sinatra albums.

Mom had an extensive wardrobe as she and my dad were social. She dressed up, even when visiting a neighbor, carrying a pitcher of frozen margaritas she whipped up in the blender. She and her friends sat back and watched the kids play as they drank, smoked, and gossiped.

My mother grew up in difficult circumstances. We were not close with her parents. Two of her brothers, Willard and Leonard, came around with their loud motorcycles and took my sister and me for rides around the neighborhood. I felt uneasy, and my dad didn't approve. Mom's brother Lloyd was in prison. We used to go visit him.

My maternal side of the family arrived in the United States from Sweden and England. I heard comments about her family being gypsies, a typical snide remark Greeks made about anyone who wasn't Greek. Because Mom grew up with little money and minimal education, she was determined to rise above that stigma through me. She worked to give me the opportunities she never had. Before a dance or acrobatics class, she said, "Try hard and pay attention. You don't know how lucky you are to be taking these classes. Nobody ever took me to a class when I was growing up."

My mother constantly enrolled me in dance classes, from tap to classical ballet. One of my earliest childhood memories is standing alone in a colossal hall where the major events in the town of Lafayette, Colorado, took place. It had wood-planked floors and a raised stage high above me. I was the only student in the class—only me and my dance teacher. My tap shoes echoed on the wooden floor as I learned new steps and combinations. Thus began a lifetime of focused physical movement.

My Sister

My sister is three years younger than me. As far back as I remember, we weren't close. We stood at a distance, her observing and me in the middle of the action. We are opposites. She is tall. I am short. She has curly hair. Mine is straight. I am extroverted. She is introverted. I was closest to our father. She was closest to our mother.

Our differences become worse during challenging times. We reconciled many of them, but our relationship is still strained. I will respect her privacy and not include details about her in this book.

Watching my friends bond with their sisters, I've wished my sister and I could count on each other, grieve and celebrate together, but that will never happen. I've accepted our relationship for what it is. I think we both have.

Growing up Greek in Salt Lake City, Utah

When I was six, my parents moved us to Salt Lake City. The Holy Trinity Greek Orthodox Church was the κέντρο or center, the place where the Greeks gathered every weekend. The church didn't hold only traditional religious services and celebrations; we gathered there for parties and other special events. Being there, we didn't feel like outsiders.

During Greek school on Saturday morning, I found myself sur-rounded by kids with names like Con (short for Constantine), Nick (short for Nikos), Pan (short for Panagiotis), and others with obvious Greek names like Sophia and Petrula. My name, Argie, is short for Αργρρω, which means silver in Greek. I felt a sense of camaraderie with the other children of Greek immigrants. We were different, hav-ing to explain our names as we navigated life and defined our identities in a city dominated by Mormons.

Next to the rather grand Greek Church, with its high-domed, hand-painted ceiling graced with angels and cherubs, exquisite, color-ful stained glass windows, and a gold pantheon of icons, was what was called the "Memorial" building. This was a functional structure, hous-ing offices and classrooms for Sunday school, a commercial kitchen, a stage, and a grand hall. On Saturday nights, everyone came to dance and listen to live bouzoukia music—lively, dance-driven rhythms that carried a sense of sorrow and cheer.

The old folks, our γιαγιάδες and παππούδες, sat and watched as the line of dancers, holding hands, circled and swayed, stepping in unison to the melancholy rhythms of the "old country." Occasionally, one of the young F.O.B.s (meaning fresh off the boat) broke from the line to go solo, moving as though possessed, dropping to his knees, arms sway-ing with the beat of the music overhead, fingers snapping, and head dropped, looking at the floor. The crowd showed their approval with cries of "Opa, opa!"

I recall those intoxicating evenings with all of my senses. The taste of lemon chicken baked in oregano, pastitsio, the Greek version of spaghetti bolognese, laced with cinnamon and clove, and topped with a velvety bechamel sauce. We ate delectable spanakopita and tiropita triangles stuffed with spinach, dill, and cheese, folded neatly with filo wrapping and brushed with butter to brown the outer layers, creating a dainty crunch when you bit into them. After dinner, cigarette smoke dominated and hovered over the gathering.

Later in the evening, the alcohol kicked in and coaxed the older folks into dancing. Once they had abandoned themselves on the dance floor, they dropped back into their chairs, sweating, huffing, dabbing themselves with white handkerchiefs. Their sweat smelled of Old Spice cologne and mothballs from the old wool suits they wore that came out of storage for the night. I imagined they must have brought them from Greece along with the rest of their belongings when they made the voyage to the United States.

A group of us kids scuttled together in a huddle, moving around the hall or behind the stage where the band played. We whispered about the other kids, silly things, like so-and-so started wearing nylons, but her mom still didn't let her shave her legs. "Did you see? Didn't the hair look funny, curled and smashed under the pantyhose!" We shared secrets and did mischievous things, like sneaking a highball of whiskey we sipped and pretended to enjoy. Sometimes we ventured outdoors to spy on the people who had stepped out for a heated conversation, a kiss, or to smoke a cigarette.

The Impressions of Physical Activity

Salt Lake City offered more physical fitness options than Lafayette. Besides dance classes, I learned unusual, exotic positions in what was called a contortionist class. I didn't understand the point of getting into those positions. Mom and my teacher encouraged me to persevere. Standing straight and stretching my arms overhead, I bent my entire body backwards, and dropped my hands on the floor behind me. They nudged me, saying, "Yes, yes, of course you can do it." My teacher urged me to walk my hands in and inch my fingers closer and closer to my heels until I touched them. My mother laughed and clapped with excitement. I knew I was doing something special and somewhat unusual because my mother and teacher were delighted with my progress.

Celebrity fitness coach Jack LaLanne had one of the first instructional exercise programs on TV. The opening lines went something like, "Here is a man who will show you how to feel better and look better so you can live longer." I thought that sounded like a good idea, so I focused and paid attention to the show. Jack LaLanne's every move captivated my mother. We sat on our rubber mats in front of the TV, using thick, squishy, blue rubber bands to assist us in the exercises. Mom told me she had specially ordered them from Jack LaLanne himself.

We followed Jack's instructions and demonstrations with serious intent. I admired his precision and how he pointed his toes. Jack wore tight stretchy pants with stirrups and a tight-fitting, short-sleeved V-neck shirt that revealed his muscular arms. In a distinct, staccato rhythm, he counted reps with vigor. "One! Two! Three!" motivational cues that helped us make it to the end of a workout he called *Firmnastics*. I was eight. I didn't realize it then, but my workouts with Jack were creating imprints, or samskaras, paving the way for my future.

To my sheer, squealing glee, my parents installed a professional, smooth, built-in trampoline. It hovered over a hole in the backyard I helped my dad dig out. We drenched the hard ground with water, turning dirt to mud, and shoveled it out until the hole was deep enough. I found a book of trampoline tricks and moves and set out to learn them. I learned to flip and twist and turn in the air. We had contests, and the neighborhood children gathered to take part. Mom forced me to take piano lessons when what I wanted was to be outside on my enormous trampoline. I saw the heads of my friends appear as they jumped, waiting for me outside as I sat obediently, my hands on the ivory keys, next to my Swedish teacher and her metronome clicking away. If I had it my way, everything I did would have been physical.

My mother took me to the roller derby, an event that took place in a large building that held a circular, slanted wooden track. The speed the skaters attained mesmerized me, crouching, crossing one leg over the other, swinging their arms from side to side, making it look effortless. They passed one another and knocked their competitors down with a quick jerk of an elbow without losing control. After seeing them, I begged my parents for a pair of roller skates.

My skates had silver metal, a toe and heel grip, two metal pieces that clamped onto my shoes, and a special key to tighten the grip around the ball of the foot. They ruined my black and white saddle oxfords, leaving an indentation that never went away, but I didn't care. I skated everywhere in the neighborhood, passing everyone who was walking to school. I went down the hill in front of our house as fast as possible, becoming braver and faster each time. The skates didn't have brakes. I figured out how to stop by squatting down and tumbling straight onto a neighbor's lawn. Skating taught me the joy of speeding through space and how to go fast without fear. I learned something different from each game or sport I played.

I used colored chalk to create perfect geometric shapes on the sidewalk for hopscotch and gathered smooth, multi-colored gummy Hoppy Taws. I stayed hopping on one foot from box to box for as long as I wanted. In learning balance, I found I stayed steady for long periods if I practiced. I spent hours on end mastering control of the Hoppy Taw. You had to throw it onto one of the numbered geometric shapes and swiftly kick it or pick it up, depending on which version of the game we played. Besides improving my balance, playing hopscotch taught me coordination and agility.

My friends and I were kids in constant motion, delighting in the freedom to explore and escape on our bikes that we rode across Salt Lake City. We relished the rush of adrenaline, jumping off scary high places like trees in the neighboring apple orchard, balconies, and roofs. After school and on breaks, we tied our sweaters around the multi-level bars on the playground of the elementary school. With one leg bent over the bar and arms clenched under the leg, we used our other leg to kick and propel ourselves around the bar at dizzying speeds, twirling as fast as possible. The speed of spinning to the point of dizziness on those monkey bars was such a thrill.

Learning to swim, dive, and move through water—a distinct feeling from moving through the air—gave me another dimension in which to experience my body. However, learning how to swim wasn't sufficient. My mother insisted I go through training to become a lifeguard.

My mom hired a Swedish swim instructor whose accent made it hard to understand her. Not knowing half of what she was saying, I mastered the swim strokes, from breaststroke to butterfly, and treaded water for what felt like an hour. My mother watched me and made sure I did everything I was told. I imagined she had wanted to take swimming classes as a young girl, but they had been cost-prohibitive. She constantly reminded me of my good fortune. "Argie, take advantage of these opportunities. I never had them growing up. We were too poor." Her words made me want to work harder. To think that all Mom had to play with when she was little were things like sticks and rocks saddened me.

Mom, my sister, and I frequented the unheated public pools during the summer months. The cold water was refreshing. Surrounded by crowds of children diving and splashing, yelling with joy was exhilarating and fun. I loved to dive, doing jackknives and backflips. If there was a high dive, I was usually the only girl to jump off of it. All it took to send me up the ladder was another kid daring me to leap. Off the board I went with a handstand or twisty dive.

The Great Salt Lake was nearby. It was a vast body of water, unlike today. I floated in the ultra-buoyant, warm, salty water. We spent the day in the lake along with the tiny shrimp-like creatures that swam with us. Afterward, we climbed into the back of the station wagon, exhausted, covered in salt, skin stinging from the sunburn we got every time. People rarely used sunscreen in those days.

On the way home, we'd stop at the only store in the remote desert area that surrounded the vast lake. We drank root beer floats out of frosty mugs, and Mom treated us to multi-colored striped saltwater taffy they made right there in the store. The shiny metal bars pulled the colored bands of saltwater taffy in all directions, much like the contortionist classes and physical pursuits stretched me.

Standing tall in Mountain Pose, Tadasana, I am about to begin my journey through life. I'm connecting not only to the surface of the earth, but even deeper down below the surface into the mantle and beyond to the core, connecting to my Earth Star Chakra. I am establishing roots, a foundation that will give me stability through the years to come. I am a child, young and unafraid. The seeds of my future are being planted through my body's twists and turns and the wheels of my roller skates. Little sprouts are emerging as I play on the trampoline with Dad, stretch with Mom in front of the television, glide through water, move as fast as possible on the neighborhood streets, and have adventures with my family, friends, and kin. I am leaning into the things I like to do, noticing that I love to experience life through the physical body. I'm aware of the strength and potential I possess. My family gives me encouragement and love. They focus on me and provide every opportunity for me to grow and blossom. I'm beginning my yearly journeys around the sun. I bask in its warmth, and I thrive as I absorb its life-giving energy.

2. Shock

He who learns must suffer. And even in our sleep, pain that cannot forget falls drop by drop upon the heart until, in our own despair, against our will, comes wisdom to us by the awful grace of God.

—Aeschylus

Volcano Pose
Urdhva Hastasana

Urdhva means upward, hasta means hands, and asana means pose. You move out of the stillness of Mountain Pose into Volcano Pose by inhaling deeply as you separate your hands from your heart. In one continuous sweeping movement, you begin by lowering your hands down to your sides, sustaining the movement by extending your arms out to the sides and upward until the palms meet directly overhead. Your gaze, your energy, and your inhalation follow the movement, all pausing at the apex. The entire body feels fully extended and lifted as it rises from its roots.

Stellar Gateway Chakra
Vyomanga ~ Heavenly Being

A brilliant golden color, the Stellar Gateway Chakra connects us to the divine—to the universe, the planets, the stars, and the sky. It's the highest of the chakras, representing the gateway to Source (God, the Universe). If you reach your hands above your head, you'll find the space where Source lives.

The Crash

A plane falls from the sky, smoke and debris trailing behind it. It is headed toward Mt. Fuji. Air currents reaching 75 miles per hour cause BOAC Flight 911, a Boeing 707, to crash into the mountainside. One hundred twenty-four people die. The cause: in-flight breakup due to severe clear-air turbulence.

I lounged on the mauve mohair sofa in my pink flannel nightgown, watching my Saturday morning TV shows and cartoons. My parents were on a trip, so I took advantage of the babysitter not paying much attention to me or my little sister. If the babysitter told me to quit being lazy and get up, I wouldn't listen. Everybody said I was headstrong—even at eleven, almost twelve. They were right.

The babysitter brought in the local paper, *The Salt Lake Tribune*, and set it on the floor in front of me.

During the next TV commercial, I picked it up. An article caught my eye—a plane crash in Japan on the sacred volcano Mt. Fuji. The victims were yet to be identified.

Hmmm. My parents were somewhere in Japan on a Thermo King Truck Refrigeration awards trip. My dad had sold enough units to qualify. The top salesmen had gone.

My parents' itinerary was on the floor in front of me. I was sure it wasn't their flight—it couldn't be—but I checked it anyway. Then, my Uncle Jack, my dad's brother, and my Aunt Clara arrived at the house. They walked in and sat down at the far end of the long L-shaped sofa. My uncle looked at my sister and me. "Girls, I don't know how to tell you this, but your folks were on that plane." With that sentence, I felt like my heart and lungs were being torn apart and crushed by metal jaws. I could not breathe.

The next thing I knew, I was in a strange bed at my aunt and uncle's house, sobbing, alone with nobody to console me. I was asking myself, "Who is going to see me go to junior high school next year?" A profound and painful sense of loss crept deep down into the core of my being and made itself at home. It felt tight around my heart.

The subsequent memory that crystallizes is of me and my Aunt Clara shopping for the dress I wore for the funeral. I remember the dress perfectly—Victorian style with a high neck, long sleeves, and a gathered, high-fitted empire bodice. It fell just below my knees. The garment was black, under the dress code of a traditional Greek Orthodox funeral, but featured tiny white polka-dots. I stared at the fabric during the service and thought that if everyone was supposed to wear only black, it wasn't proper for my dress to have little white dots. It didn't seem right. Nothing seemed right. I kept staring down at those white dots.

I felt the pain of losing my parents manifest as tightness, a stiffening of my body. It was difficult for me to move. I sat there and hung my head to avoid looking at people's faces. All of them stared at me. They tilted their heads, squinted their eyes, and burst into tears if I looked at them. They must have been thinking, *Poor little girl, now she is an orphan. What will happen to her?*

Mourners wept at the funeral, some people with their private muted tears, while others burst out with screams, wailing, arms clutching at the casket. I sat there in my own little world, unable to grasp the tragedy that engulfed me. I knew I was in a state of shock, feeling deep, deep, deep grief. Looking back so many years later, I understand my grief as an unwanted, unintentional rebirth, one involving forceps dragging me into another world, so different from the last. I was no longer the same lucky, carefree girl. I felt thrust into a serious, grave adulthood.

The funeral was closed-casket. I never saw my parents' faces again, probably a good thing considering the circumstances. Uncle Mike, who identified my parents, said that their bodies and faces were almost unrecognizable. He said my father had a huge wound in his chest that almost split his body in half and a broken nose. My mother's face was smashed pretty badly. I guess my uncle felt compelled to tell my sister and me what he saw. After everything, they were our parents.

Mom was nervous before leaving for the trip. She had worried about flying ever since she had invited a palm reader to our house. I was in the ironing room. Mother was obsessed with ironing. Not only did we have an ironing board but also a mangle, a special machine you sat in front of and fed in a sheet or pillowcase and watched it come out on the other side, hot and pressed. I stood next to it, overhearing the palm reader tell my mom she would die in a plane crash at a young age. She read my sister's palm and told her she would have a difficult life. Me? She said, "You will be very lucky and have an interesting life."

Imagine my mother hearing a prediction so grim with her daughters present.

During the time the palm reader came to visit, Dad flew our family to Las Vegas every weekend in his Cessna 180. He loved taking us up in the plane to look at the Wasatch Mountains surrounding Salt Lake. He pushed the nose down just right, so the airplane dropped faster than we did. For a few seconds, our seats didn't seem to hold us—our bodies felt light, almost floating—and we'd laugh as a tissue magically drifted out of the box in midair.

Mom knew she and Dad had to take multiple flights on the trip to Japan. It must have terrified her to consider she might die. The palm reader was right. Not long after she made her prediction, at 27, Mom died in an airplane crash.

After the palm reader predicted my parents' death, I believed in powerful, cosmic forces directing our lives. I spent years navigating the unpleasant feelings of uncertainty. We are not in control. The palm reader's prediction scared and intrigued me. I had to know more. Later in my life, I became intimate with astrology to make sense of my history and embrace my destiny. I would not reconcile my life through examining the past or understanding myself psychologically. The positioning and movement of the Sun, Moon, planets, and stars became my reference point for the events in my life—the personalities I encountered, the relationships I formed, and my path.

After the funeral, Mom's relatives poured in, gathered her clothes and most of her belongings, and carried them away. Nobody asked me if that was okay. I was too numb to say or do anything about it. It made me sad her dresses were no longer hanging in the same place. When I slid back the closet door and peered inside, except for a few dangling wire hangers, it was empty. I turned to open the drawer in her dresser to see if they had taken the little jewelry box, the one with her costume earrings and necklaces that matched her outfits. It was gone. I had always loved trying on her plastic button earrings and parading around in her high-heeled pumps. At least they had saved her aquamarine ring and slim platinum watch for me. I still have the watch. I take it out and look at it, but I have never worn it. It was with her on the trip. They retrieved it from her wrist when they recovered her body.

Even so young, I knew then I couldn't stay in that dark grief for too long. It was unbearable. I would die of heartbreak. I needed help. A few days after Mom's relatives emptied her closet, I stood alone in the middle of the field in front of our house. I gazed up towards Mount Olympus, rising majestically, presiding over Salt Lake City with its craggy, textured face and jagged peak. I felt a sudden disconnect from everything, as if someone had turned off the electricity, and everything became eerily silent. It felt like a giant eraser was circling me, rapidly smudging away people, emotional attachments, and connections to the spaces I inhabited, like my home, bedroom, bathroom, and schoolroom. I felt detached from the world.

I looked up at the mountain. A question welled up out of nowhere, a loud voice in my head asked, "Who am I? What am I really doing here?" I didn't feel like it came from the same little girl I knew as me, who had lived in my body for the past 12 years. This was my first spiritual experience, one of not being of the world I knew, but of something far beyond. It wasn't particularly joyous or blissful; it was a soothing presence telling me I wasn't alone. I'm unsure how long I stood there or what happened next, but I recall the experience perfectly. I think of it often, and when I do, I feel the presence of someone or something divine.

In many traditions—especially Eastern ones—a tragedy is viewed as a gift, a doorway for the soul to grow. At the time of my parents' passing, I couldn't see it that way. My anchors were gone, and nothing would be the same. If anyone told me my loss was a "gift," I would have thought they were out of their mind. It took years—decades—to even consider that perspective.

Mount Fuji is a sacred volcano. I didn't visit it until almost forty years after the crash, when I was finally able to bring gratitude to my grief. The morning after I arrived, I sat down for breakfast in the hotel restaurant. Through the large picture window, there it was—my first time seeing it in person. Guests at other tables had angled their chairs toward the view as if drawn to it.

When the server came to take my order, he noticed me staring and said, "You know, it's rare to see it so clearly. It's usually hidden behind mist and clouds." I almost told him my parents had died on that mountain in a plane crash. But I stopped myself. I didn't want his joy to vanish or for him to regret his kind words.

That day, the mountain revealed itself in full splendor—enormous, commanding, sacred. This was the last sight my parents saw before the pilot flew closer for a better view, a choice that ended their lives. Tears welled up as I looked at the place that swallowed them, taking their lives from me so many years ago.

I wondered: what does it symbolize to die by crashing into a revered, sacred volcano? Was there a message hidden in it? I began to wonder what good I would make from the loss.

The Stellar Gateway Chakra represents a heavenly being, a connection to the greater universe beyond the physical plane. Because of the tragedy I experienced, I searched for answers. Why did this happen to me? Who am I as an orphan, alone in the world? What could fill this numb, empty shell of a body now that the love, care, sense of security, source of wisdom, and guidance my parents had provided for me had disappeared? A gateway began to open. All I lost would be replaced, but with what? The quest to find the answers became my spiritual journey.

Some people say it takes a painful loss to make us evolve and look beyond our familiar, mundane existence. Without hardship, we fixate on the insatiable, never-ending pursuits of ego and gratification. As in Volcano Pose, I was reaching up, searching beyond my physical self for guidance. I held my inhalation and paused— numb and afraid of what awaited me.

3. Survival

Our greatest glory is not in never falling, but in rising every time we fall.

—Oliver Goldsmith

Standing Forward Bend
Uttanasana

Uttana means intense. Asana means pose. It is a posture used to relieve stress and soothe the nervous system. The pose begins with an extended exhalation that endures throughout a forward dive, a folding of the body in half from the hips. The arms initiate the movement, beginning with the separation of the palms, which open to face downward as the arms sweep gracefully outward and descend until the hands reach the ground, just outside the feet. Fingers and toes, all twenty of them, align in a single row.

Heart Chakra
Anahata ~ unhurt

Emerald green, the heart chakra allows us to feel love and compassion. It governs forgiveness, emotional safety, hope, trust, and joy. The heart informs the brain through the messages it transmits. Grief causes the heart chakra to contract, hardening the walls that surround and protect it. It is located in the center of the chest.

After the Crash

Aunt Clara, Uncle Jack, and their two kids, George and Dea, moved into our house. This arrangement lasted for two years until my Uncle Mike took us. Since my dad and Uncle Mike both owned small planes, they made a pact that if anything ever happened to either of them, they vowed to take care of each other's kids. He was divorced and single, making him unable to get full custody of me and my sister until he found a new wife.

Aunt Clara did her best. She was prone to migraines. I overheard comments from people saying she was "high-strung." The tall, striking woman with a low voice, who pronounced words with precision, was impeccably dressed, with no wrinkles in her clothing. She didn't wear perfume; she smelled clean. Her waist was tiny and her hips large, perfect for the style of the '60s with the cinched-in dress and full skirts. She had thick hair, cut short in a neat, cropped style, that never fell out of place. On special occasions, she wore lipstick but no other makeup. I never saw her when she wasn't groomed. Even in the morning, she sat in her pale pink dressing gown and robe with her metal pot of black coffee, which she drank as she read the Bible.

Aunt Clara struggled to take on two new "daughters," although I perceived a genuine sense of duty in her. She had loved my dad like a little brother. She often spoke fondly of "Billy," so I think she decided she was going to teach his girls everything she knew how to do. We learned to sew, make spanakopita and baklava, make a proper bed, clean the house, and sit and act like "ladies."

As one of my dad's older brothers, Uncle Jack resembled him most. Unlike my dad, he never dressed up in fancy suits or golf clothes. He was a simple man, wearing a fresh white short-sleeved T-shirt every day, tucked into his gray cotton trousers. He was a cook, not a chef, working in restaurants and factories since he was a young man. College wasn't an option for him. The family had just arrived from Greece when he was born, unable to afford tuition.

Uncle Jack needed to work to survive and help the family. Like clockwork, he left at 4 a.m. to attend to his industrial kitchen in a factory on the outskirts of Salt Lake City. The three girls (my sister, cousin, and I) visited on the weekend to help peel dozens of eggs or shell peas. The kitchen was sterile and tidy, filled with enormous stainless steel pots and pans. There, my uncle made enough food to feed dozens of employees.

He had "Jack's Specials" written on the chalkboard at the entrance to the buffet counter where the employees lined up for their lunch, featuring dishes like SOS (shit on a shingle), a creamy white sauce with bits of beef over toast, chicken cutlets with peas and mashed potatoes, or versions of my grandmother's Greek dishes he must have learned from her. The workers loved him. His mood was usually good. When he came home from work, he took a nap, ate dinner, slept, and started over again the next morning. Jack was nice to me, but I never had any meaningful conversations with him. We didn't talk about how I was feeling. I'm sure he knew the conversation would be difficult, considering I had lost my parents.

While living with Aunt Clara and Uncle Jack, I was in a consistent state of shock—going through the motions of being a student, trying not to think about my parents, was hard. Being forced to attend school every day didn't help. The only things that took my mind off Mom and Dad were physical activity or thinking about boys.

Schoolwork was easy for me, even though I skipped many classes. I preferred to spend my time in the gym. I became a competitive gymnast. The brutal discipline, the falls (I think I lost my virginity when I fell on the balance beam), bruises, triumphs, and humiliations proved to be helpful in the aftermath of my parents' death—intense enough to take my mind off my loss.

I rose to compete as a high-level AAU gymnast. Some officials approached my coach, Ms. Alvey, at a regional gymnastics meet where I had performed well. They asked her if I was going to continue competing. They saw potential in me to train for the Olympic Games. I felt eager about the idea because I loved training, learning tough moves, and pleasing my coach. While competing in the Olympics wasn't in the cards, those years of gymnastics gave me focus, determination, and discipline that served me later in life.

When I wasn't practicing gymnastics, I was outdoors. On most winter Saturdays, my sister and I loaded ourselves and our ski equipment into a bus that came by to pick up the neighborhood children who had signed up for the winter ski program. In those days, the skis were long. Everyone recommended they be as long as the length of the ground up to your fingertips with your arm stretched above your head. We used heavy, chunky leather ski boots with laces and liners.

It was all so new and exciting. It helped me forget my pain. I was learning a new, exhilarating, and tough sport. I loved seeing how I improved each week, learning the techniques from snowplow to stem christie to parallel skiing. Many ski resorts were within driving distance of home. My favorite was Alta. Snowbird didn't even exist back then, but Brighton, Solitude, and Park City did.

If the weather was nice, I roller-skated or played hopscotch. Nobody was watching me like my mom used to. Still, I loved the focus and difficulty. I pushed myself. Through gymnastics, I developed outstanding balance and coordination that carried over to my other games and activities. I found my safe space and replaced my heartbreak with pursuing physical prowess. There was a connection between the pain of loss and my determination. It drove me and pushed me, perhaps because I felt I had nothing to lose. Even as a young girl, I felt a certain strength and determination emerging from the pain.

Competitive gymnastics took my physical propensity to another level. Dance, contortionist classes, swimming, biking, summers on the trampoline, and skiing in winter served me later, allowing me to practice and later teach yoga with an ideal foundation.

At twelve, I was prematurely pushed into adulthood. I was making my own decisions, living in the same house I had lived in with my parents, yet everything had changed. My sister, more belligerent and unhappy than ever, our cousin Dea, and I shared the larger bedroom. Our cousin George was experimenting with weed, and he kept wanting me to smoke it with him. I experimented a few times. Young and in a vulnerable state of mind, I experienced bewilderment and paranoia on marijuana. I realized the strict supervision and guidance my parents had provided were no longer there. If I wanted to get high or skip class, no one was there to stop me. My life was entirely up to me.

In Uttanasana, Standing Forward Bend, you move from an upright position into a submissive bow, becoming half as tall. The gaze shifts from looking upward in the previous posture to turning inward. You experience an intense, uncomfortable stretch throughout the entire backside of the body while pressure builds throughout the front of the torso.

At this point in my young life, I had equally lost my stature. Pain followed me to school and sat through every class. Grief hovered beside me at the gym as I learned a new routine on the uneven bars, clinging to my shoulders even when my body glided through the air. I felt like half the person I used to be—uncomfortable, under pressure—my heart bruised and tight. Grief crawled into bed with me, settled under the covers, and curled up in my heart space. It felt heavy, like lead, murky and bereft. It lashed out and extinguished any flicker of joy. The Heart Anahata Chakra was working overtime to show its love and heal me, but the road ahead was long. It would need to break through the walls closing in, drive out the darkness that had settled there, and reclaim the space as its own.

Eventually, after many repetitions of Uttanasana Forward Bend, the hamstrings, along with the muscles in the buttocks and lower back, stretch, lengthen, release, and adapt to the strain.

4. Reset

It does not matter how slow you go as long as you don't stop.

—Confucius

Half Standing Forward Bend
Ardha Uttanasana

Ardha means half, uttana means intense, and asana means pose. Inhale as you raise your head to gaze forward, but only to the point where your palms lift off the ground while your fingertips remain anchored. Tilt the sacrum to deepen the stretch, lengthening the muscles throughout the entire backside of the legs. Create a deep curve in the spine, completely changing its shape from the previous posture. Press your shoulders firmly away from your ears, allowing space for the upper chest and throat to open.

Sacral Chakra
Svadhishthana ~ dwelling place of the self

Orange is the color of the sacral chakra associated with the for-
mation of our identity. As the center of creativity, personal power,
and passion, it helps you move out of survival mode to pleasure.
Located just below the navel, it governs the surrounding space
and the physical body in that region, as is the function of all the
chakras in their respective locations.

Moving to Denver

After two years of struggling to blend our lives with those of Uncle
Jack, Aunt Clara, and their children, my sister and I left to start over
again. I think they were relieved to see us go. I had to leave my dear
friends and my gymnastics coach behind, more loss. I didn't want to
leave.

My uncle Mike had married Kathy and was ready to take over as
our legal guardian. I look back and wonder if he was also looking forward to being the executor of our estate. Boeing had paid out sizable
sums of money to the victims' families. Both my sister and I had a rather

large inheritance. A few months later, my uncle asked me for money. He needed it to serve as collateral for a new Thermo King building he was constructing. The bank wanted to see his financials. I agreed, even though his asking didn't sit right with me. It wasn't right for him to risk my money to help himself. Later, when I knew more about finances, I realized I would never have done something like that if I were in his position as my guardian and executor of my estate.

We acclimated to our new life by getting a dachshund named Schnapps and started playing family again. Everyone but my sister tried. She rebelled, got into trouble at school, and made everyone miserable with her explosive temper and sporadic moods.

Only the house was happy. A mid-century modern with a dramatic round metal fireplace in the middle of the living room, it was spacious with an open floor plan and a high ceiling. This was the '60s. The decorator Uncle Mike and Kathy hired came in with ideas to create a new environment for the new family. She brought in contemporary sleek furniture, bright acrylic paintings of sunflowers and poppies, and plexiglass tables that were perched over shag carpet. The pervading colors were white, orange, yellow, and bright lime green. The house was modern and airy, with a giant picture window looking out to the mountains. It reminded me of a house on the TV show *The Jetsons*. It was nice, but nothing could fill the void of our old life. I got by, but nothing made my sister smile. We had a lot of family counseling, and the dog soothed everyone, but it wasn't exactly a harmonious household.

A New School

I went to St. Mary's Academy, a small Catholic school on the other side of Denver. Condoleezza Rice was in my class. She was a serious student, setting the standard for the rest of us. Decades later, she became the first female African-American to be the US Secretary of State. Although the academic level at St. Mary's was higher than at my public school in Salt Lake City, I performed well and earned good grades. I adored my Spanish teacher and developed a burning interest in learning the language. It came easily to me. Little did I know, I would eventually live in a Spanish-speaking country, become fluent, and use the language for the rest of my life. I found ways to cope and acclimate to my new school.

My background in dance and gymnastics allowed me to become the head cheerleader for the affiliated boys' school called St. Regis. I choreographed our cheers, loved rehearsing, and loved going to the games. There we were, in front of the crowd, bouncing around in our red and white flared mini skirts, red monogrammed sweaters, and sneakers. We performed our cheers in unison, jumping and waving our pom-poms, screaming with the excitement of the game. The physicality of cheering and the pressure of being in sync with the other girls gave me some relief, but I had slipped into a convenient identity that wasn't me. I was going through the motions. I felt empty. My peers surrounded me, but I made only one friend. Her name was Tink Stewart. Tink smoked cigarettes and had a car. We got in trouble for smoking pot. Our friendship didn't go any further than lighting up a joint her older brother gave at the far end of the parking lot of the St. Mary's campus, where we got busted by the nuns. They had eyes everywhere.

Tink and I were kicked out of school, and I moved to George Washington Public High School, corresponding to the Hilltop neighborhood where we lived. I'm not sure where Tink went.

My First Boyfriend

Billy Goodro, regarded by my uncle as "bad news," was several years older than me. His job was selling cars at his father's dealership, requiring a suit and tie as well as persuasion. Using his car sales techniques, he sold me on our relationship. Every date, he'd arrive in a different, fancy car. Six feet tall with blonde hair and blue eyes, he wanted to go "all the way" with me. Uncle Mike stared Billy down when he came to the house. "He's too old for you," he said. My uncle and Billy conferred silently. Resisting my uncle's disapproval, Billy slammed his foot on the accelerator, screeching the tires as we drove away from our house. He laughed as he looked in the rearview mirror to see if Uncle Mike was watching.

Uncle Mike kept telling me, "Argie, stay away from that guy—he wants to get in your pants." It was uncomfortable to hear my uncle talk to me about sex, but he was right. He handled my safety. As my legal guardian, I'm sure he felt it was his duty to my parents. He was strict. I acted out—a solid student, but not the best rule follower.

Uncle Mike was right; sex was what Billy wanted. We did it on the golf course under the stars, in the different cars he borrowed from the dealership. We had sex anywhere we got away with it. I liked him, the way he smelled, his neatness, and the way he wrapped his body around mine. Being with him exhilarated me, and it freed me from the family's discomfort. I kept seeing him until I graduated from high school, and we went our separate ways.

The Coming and Going of Winter

Another thing that gave me joy and space from the loss of my parents during that time in Denver was skiing. I had learned to ski at the resorts surrounding Salt Lake City in my early childhood, but the powdery mountains of Colorado ignited my passion for the sport.

My uncle bought a one-acre lot in Frisco, Colorado, and had a prefab house installed. Our home was bright and cheerful with orange shag carpeting, big comfy sofas, and plastic bean bags for lounging. The kitchen had olive-green Formica countertops and pine cupboards. Big picture windows looked out onto the pine trees, aspen, and surrounding mountains. In those days, the late '60s, the Eisenhower Tunnel didn't exist, and we had to drive over Loveland Pass every weekend to get to Frisco. We brought our groceries from Denver because there weren't any supermarkets nearby.

We rode snowmobiles with Uncle Mike and his friends. Lake Dillon was frozen, making it easy to ride through the entire area up into the surrounding mountains, creating bobsled-like passages. At that time, snowmobiles were heavy. We were careful not to fall off, as it took hours to dig ourselves and the machine out of the snow.

I remember skiing on opening day at Keystone. We skied full days. With barely any lift lines back then, we made a lot of runs. I felt free and happy, and like gymnastics, skiing gave me a physical outlet I found to be healing. It had only been three years since the death of my parents, and life was taking me in an unforeseen direction. I had no choice but to make the best of my situation.

The memory of Dad telling me I could do anything I put my mind to stayed with me. I wanted to test if he was right and decided that instead of Miss America, I would be a master skier. Sadly, I left gymnastics behind, but the privilege of learning to ski presented itself, so that became my focus. I was learning to adapt and make the best of my situation—a skill that has served me well throughout my life. My dedication made me a lifelong avid skier with the fortune to make my home in the ski town of Vail.

Despite enjoying skiing on the weekends, my heart wasn't in it. I missed my gymnastics coach and my old friends from Salt Lake. Living in Denver, nothing evoked memories of my parents. I still longed to be close to them. Salt Lake offered reminders.

When we left Salt Lake to move to Denver with Uncle Jack and Aunt Clara, we drove by the Arctic Circle, a popular fast-food joint. It reminded me of the nights when my mom didn't want to cook. We snuggled in the car with a warm blanket on snowy evenings, Dad driving on the icy roads to get hamburgers and fries with a special sauce made of mayo and ketchup. I still make it because it reminds me of my parents. I longed for the places we went as a family.

I missed the Holy Trinity Greek Orthodox Church and the Saturday night revelry, watching the old Greek people dance and the sound of the bouzoukia music. Driving downtown Salt Lake on our way out of town, I glimpsed the Manhattan Club and remembered my parents leaving to go there for late-night drinks. Those were the days of double martinis and dancing, even in Salt Lake with the large Mormon community.

The house where I lived from six to fourteen was sold when my sister and I left. My Aunt Clara, Uncle Jack, George, and Dea moved back into their old house. The reality and the finality that my parents were not coming back seeped in more profoundly. Moving to Denver, I lost the comforting presence of my father and my mother. Kathy and Mike could never take their place.

My Aunt Kathy was the opposite of my Aunt Clara. She was young, never had children, and didn't have a clue about cooking or running a household. I think she wanted to get us off to college and out of the house as soon as possible so she and Uncle Mike could travel. They were gone a lot, anyway. Distance persisted between us as I got older. Eventually, we became closer, but I decided not to stay close to home once I graduated from George Washington High. I was only sixteen and a half when I finished high school. I was ahead on credits from the rigorous curriculum that transferred over after I was suspended from St. Mary's. I had a desire to complete that phase of my life, assert my independence, and head to Los Angeles. Loyola University accepted me, and I drove my AMC Pacer away from Denver toward the City of Angels.

I couldn't believe Mike and Kathy allowed me to leave. I felt they were indifferent to me. I was living on my own, as lonely as ever, but I developed coping skills. My innate determination and inner guidance system began directing me.

I knew I had to move on from Denver. I was acutely aware of my autonomy and independence. No one else remained. I didn't relate to my sister. My aunts and uncles had done what they could to get me through the mourning period; they had fulfilled their responsibility. My adventurous spirit was emerging. I was getting more comfortable with the sense of loss I would never shake off. My survival instincts kicked in. I was about to be put to the test as a teenager on her own in the buzzing City of Los Angeles.

As in Ardha Uttanasana, I was attempting to look forward, to see a revised future for myself, a new timeline (a term you hear often these days). This required significant effort that stretched my perceived limitations, leading me into unknown territory. I was learning a new language, improving my skiing, and adapting to a new school in an unfamiliar city. As in the previous posture, the hamstrings here are lengthened and stretched, but more intensely. This posture prepares the body for deeper forward bends. In this pose, the sacrum changes direction—it becomes the pivot point. At this time in my life, the sacral chakra came into prominence in the form of a sexual awakening. I also experienced a shift from survival mode to one of growing personal power. I was developing the ability to overcome loss, lift my head, and gaze toward the future.

5. Zest

Love the life you live. Live the life you love.

—Bob Marley

Plank Pose
Dandasana

Danda means staff. Asana means pose. Your exhalation carries you through the jumping motion that lands you firmly yet gently on the toes. Your body is now parallel to the ground, and your gaze is straight down at the earth. You are now holding the weight of your entire body with your hands positioned directly below the shoulders. The muscles of the front side of the body, especially those of the core, are engaged throughout the movement, supporting the lower back.

Solar Plexus Chakra
Manipura ~ lustrous gem

Yellow like the sun, the Solar Plexus Chakra governs things such as personal freedom and choice, confidence, authenticity, and personal control. It is the source of vitality associated with our ability to take action based on inner wisdom. It is located in the pit of the stomach, above the navel.

My Persian Family

After I got to LA, I decided to explore and meet the real Angelenos rather than hang out with the immature students on the Loyola Marymount campus. Whereas the other students on campus had their parents to answer to and watch over them, constantly calling and checking in, I was free. Being around them made me realize how much I had matured after the death of my parents. I was developing survival instincts after they passed—fearless, as I had nothing to lose. It sparked a playful desire to live life to the fullest.

I focused much of my life as a student on learning my Greek heritage. The older members of my family, the first-generation Greeks, didn't get an education. They didn't study mythology or know much about Greek history. Peasants from the Greek countryside, after they arrived in America, their focus was on providing for their families.

My elders didn't have the answers to the questions I had about our cultural history. I remember hearing their conversations. "Provide for your children, and help them go to college." As my grandparents and parents wished, I took advantage of what higher learning offered. Admittedly, I didn't take school as seriously as I took my social life. Los Angeles made it easy to get distracted from my studies.

The hottest trends in fashion and fitness were being born in Los Angeles, and I wanted to be a part of the scene. Talented, creative people came to pursue acting careers in television and cinema. Everyone in LA was attractive, tan, and fit. The air buzzed with cinematic glitz and glamour.

Cameron was the first person I met when I ventured off campus. I found a dance studio on La Cienega Boulevard. The class was full of professional dancers, or at least that's how it seemed to me. I was swept up by the music and the skillful moves of the dancers surrounding me. *Wow*, I thought, *this is Hollywood, and I'm a part of it*! I walked out of class, flushed and floating. I was high on my first experience dancing alongside people who looked like movie stars. After class, feeling sweaty and exhilarated, I walked next door and into a store called Jeans West. Immediately, an attractive young man approached me and introduced himself. His real name was Camran, a beautiful Persian name, but he changed the spelling to Cameron. Little did I know that meeting him would lead me to discover the intricacies of Persian culture.

Cameron looked like the folk-rock musician Cat Stevens—long, wavy hair framing his face, a full beard softening his features, and eyes that carried the same soulful, faraway depth. Cameron dressed in fitted, faded bell-bottom blue jeans, likely because he worked for Jeans West. He opened new stores for them. Not only did he look and dress like Cat Stevens, but he was also an accomplished musician. He played the guitar and cello.

Some years later, he opened a violin shop on the popular Melrose Avenue. Musicians brought their violins and other stringed instruments to be tuned and repaired. They sold violins made by his father, Camille. He built them in the back room. I enjoyed watching Camille at work. He moved mindfully and slowly, smoothing the wood, carefully carving the graceful curves of the violin's body. His pace drove Cameron crazy. Having worked under pressure at Jeans West to open as many stores as quickly as possible, Cameron didn't like to "waste time" like his father.

I, however, appreciated Camille. From observing him, I learned not to rush an artistic process such as violin making. It requires precision and a step-by-step approach: fitting, filing, and gluing together carved wooden pieces, assembling them to see how they fit and making adjustments.

It didn't take long after meeting Cameron for him to introduce me to his family. They taught me many phrases, words, and songs in Farsi. Somehow, it amused them to hear me speak Farsi, especially phrases like, "Did you fart?"

They must have seen me alone in the world—no parents, a sister I wasn't close to, navigating a big city like LA at a young age. Guity, Cameron's mother, cooked a big Persian meal every Sunday. Cameron and I, his sister, Leyla, her husband, Kambiz, and their younger brother, Sam (or Siamak), crowded around the dining table, devouring everything Guity made. I had never tasted Persian food.

They shared with me the customs of their kitchen. One of my favorites was putting a raw egg yolk in the center of hot, long-grain rice, then stirring it with a fork so the heat of the rice cooked it. After being flipped upside down from the pan onto the serving plate, the rice revealed a golden glaze of toasted butter and an irresistibly crunchy crust. The dish was garnished with a sprinkle of sumac and dried lime, adding a tart, heavenly flavor.

Guity cooked many Persian dishes I enjoyed. There was the fragrant stew called Ghormeh Sabzi made of kidney beans, meat, and green herbs. One of my favorites was the traditional Chelow Kabab over fluffy saffron-infused rice. And Baghali Polo, a luxurious rice dish with fava beans and fresh dill. In her charming broken English, she graciously demonstrated each step, showing me how to make her recipes.

Cameron, Leyla, and I traveled to London and explored the mecca of fashion in the '70s. Biba, the London fashion store, had recently opened. Leyla was a fashionista. We would spend hours putting together outfits with the streamlined fitted hats of the '20s adorned with feathers and lace, high-heeled chunky shoes, fabulous pins, and brooches. I don't think there has ever been a store like Biba to this day! Six floors of fabulous fashion in an Art Deco building. There was a buzz of excitement and a frenzy to scoop up as many fantastic pieces as possible. Customers couldn't get enough of it. Everywhere you looked, there was something you had to have.

After marathon-like shopping, we rode the metal-caged elevator up to the tea salon, where a domed ceiling painted like the sky hovered over exhausted shoppers from all over the world, most of them already wearing their new purchases. They just couldn't wait!

On that same trip, we travelled by train—Biba purchases head-to-toe, oozing sophisticated chic—to Kent. Cameron and Leyla had relatives there, part of the Persian diaspora as well, finding themselves in a house simply called "The Garden House," no other address needed. It was the first time I had seen a real English manor and garden. The house was enormous and the garden stunning, discreetly controlled and tamed, yet wild with flowers everywhere, richly nourished by the misty, damp air. Everything was old-world, charming, and beautiful: the tableware, silver, the furniture, and books strewn everywhere. Nothing like this existed in Salt Lake City or Denver.

I took it all in and asked questions about everything. I didn't want to seem like an unworldly orphan from a mining town in Colorado, yet I felt a strong desire to become more cultured and worldly. My time with Cameron and Leyla would be mostly isolated to these early days in Los Angeles, but our paths would cross over the coming decades.

Lisa Keeper

Lisa Keeper was from Houston, Texas. She looked like a doll with peaches and cream complexion, dark auburn hair, and shiny eyes rimmed with thick dark lashes. She was constantly laughing and smiling. Lisa had a flair for dressing. I guess that's why she came to LA to attend the Fashion Institute of Design and Merchandising (FIDM) downtown. I had given up on Loyola Marymount. It was dull compared to the vibrant fashion scene of Los Angeles. My aunt and uncle didn't mind that I wanted to change direction. We rarely talked. I enrolled at FIDM and spent the next two years there, receiving my associate's degree.

Lisa had her cute little mom named Dolly. She came with her from Houston to help her daughter find the right apartment and roommate, who turned out to be me. When Dolly went back to Houston after getting Lisa settled in, she called her almost every day. They chatted as if they hadn't talked in ages. Listening to them, I wished I could call my mother for advice and share all I was discovering with her.

Westwood was the perfect place for Lisa and me to live. Downtown and Beverly Hills were only a thirty-minute drive. Westwood Village was full of students from UCLA. There were coffee shops and cute boutiques. Our two-bedroom furnished apartment was quite upscale. The building had a pool we often used, though not for more than a quick dip. It served as a place for entertaining boys, meeting people, and wearing our colorful bathing suits, coordinated flowery cover-ups, and wooden platform sling sandals.

Fred Slatten Shoes

That leads me to the shoes. I was a shoe fanatic as far back as I could remember. When they told us at FIDM that part of the two-year Associates of Arts program meant finding a job in the fashion industry, I got a job at Fred Slatten Shoes. This was no ordinary shoe store. Nestled between the buzzing Troubadour nightclub and celebrity-laden Dan Tana's restaurant on Santa Monica Boulevard, designer Fred Slatten's signature was platform shoes and only platform shoes.

Fred Slatten was an artist, a shoe genius, and a visionary. He was tall, trim, reserved, probably in his 60s, and nice enough, but totally consumed with his creations. He sketched new designs when he wasn't obsessively rearranging the shoe displays. None of the girls (there were just three of us) knew anything about him. As far as we could see, he didn't have any family around or anything else going on in his life. His shoes were his babies; he loved them and was constantly coming up with new designs and ideas. They were the only thing he cared about. Sometimes, he hid behind the black velvet curtain that partitioned off the back room and listened to the comments customers made about his shoes. He loved to hear the people oooh and ahhhh over them.

Two bright, sparkling disco balls would spotlight the latest high-as-heaven custom creations like starlets as they rotated on black velvet circular displays in each of the shopfront windows. Cars slowed down on the boulevard just to get a glimpse of the displays. Elton John, Diana Ross, Cher, and many other big stars shopped for their shoes at Fred Slatten, and I got to help them choose which ones to buy. The store was more of a shoe museum with every pair perfectly curated and positioned along black walls and illuminated with track lighting. Every wall in the store was painted black. Lush carpets and animal skins covered the floor.

Fred found and commissioned artists to hand-paint one-of-a-kind fantasy scenes and designs on high wooden platforms. Some had themes such as Carmen Miranda, with soles covered in intricate, colorful designs complete with feathers and gems. Others were satin with platform toes and high heels covered in waves of pearls and pink, blue, and amethyst rhinestones, rising to varying heights depending on how tall you wanted to be and how much risk you were willing to take to balance on them. You had the Baby Sister 3-inch heel, Little Sister 5-inch heel, and Big Sister 7-inch heel. And then there were the fabulous brown, black, and red leather boots with art all the way up the leg.

We wore high-waisted gabardine pants, tight enough to show off our figures and hemmed to just the right length to let the shoes peek out, and a silk blouse in coordinated colors to go with the pants, soft beige, dusty rose, teal blue—very elegant. You had to be cute to work there, and you had to have nice feet to model Fred's creations.

Nicole, pretty, fresh-faced, voluptuous, and never without lip gloss, worked there. She was dating O.J. Simpson. He rarely came into the store; instead, he drove up, leaned across the seat, and glanced into the store to let her know he was waiting. She would hurry out and hop into his car. Sometimes she came to work with a bruised lip. Later, he married another Nicole . . .

Bikram 1974

A friend told me about a new type of class that was being offered in the basement of an office building on the corner of Wilshire Boulevard and Beverly Drive in Beverly Hills. It was called yoga. I had never heard of it. She had also been a competitive gymnast growing up and had heard the class was incredibly challenging. I couldn't believe it was that difficult. If I could do a walkover on the balance beam (considered rather difficult in the '60s), then I was sure I could do this thing called yoga. She told me to wear a leotard, no tights, but it couldn't be green because the instructor, Bikram, hated green.

I arrived wearing a flowy, flowery silk patchwork skirt with a jagged hemline over my shiny light blue leotard and platform shoes. I parked my brand-new tan Mercedes 350 SL convertible nearby. (I had convinced my uncle to turn over my entire inheritance, and I was spending it like it would never run out.) I entered the corner office building and bought a series of classes before even giving this yoga thing a try. I had a feeling I was going to like it.

The studio itself was a large carpeted room with floor-to-ceiling mirrors on two sides. Bright fluorescent lighting gave it an office feel, and it felt hot, damp, and sweaty. Bikram Choudhury commanded the space, perched on a pile of cushions, watching everyone. He broke into songs from his native India, as if to remind himself of his origins . . . or perhaps he was homesick? He had a sweet, lyrical singing voice and a harsh, imposing voice when he was spewing out instructions for the asanas (postures). It was 1974, and Bikram was just getting started. He had recently arrived from India, and he was on a mission.

Bikram recognized my ability to do well with the asanas. After a few weeks of classes, he took me aside and told me I could become a yoga instructor. I was required to attend class six days a week for two years, one and a half hours per day the first year and three and a half hours the second. Little did I know I was to become the first of thousands of teachers he trained.

Taking a Bikram class was heaven to me, not solely because of the yoga. There were celebrities such as the Smothers Brothers, Quincy Jones, and his pregnant wife, Peggy Lipton. Raquel Welch, with her tiny waist, was there, soaking it all in. A year later, she did one of the first instructional yoga videos, copying everything as Bikram did, except she changed the name of Balancing Stick to T-pose. (Bikram sued her, but it's unclear who won.)

Juliet Prowse, known for having the best legs since Betty Grable, was a regular. I had seen her perform in Las Vegas on a trip with my parents when I was ten. My dad arranged for us to go backstage to her dressing room and meet her. I thought, "Wow, if my dad could see me now with these television and movie stars!"

Bikram forcefully commanded the class, and everyone readily adhered. He ran an extremely strict class. Nobody was allowed to even touch their "costumes," as he liked to call them.

"Hands by your sides between postures! Don't talk! Focus! Try harder! Listen to me, and I will not only change your body, get rid of those cottage cheese thighs, but I will change your life."

Everyone obeyed him, hanging on his every word and pushing themselves until they were panting and drenched in sweat. Bikram would yell if we didn't try hard enough, pushing us to our limits and beyond. He watched everyone closely, totally focused the entire time, scanning the room with his penetrating gaze. There was "no talking" and "no slacking," not even for a second. He gave one hundred percent of himself to teaching. He expected everyone in the class to respond with the same effort.

"Please join the front row," Bikram invited me to stand in front of him alongside the fittest people in the class, including my new friend, Linda. I met her early on. She was ten years older than me, but you wouldn't know it with her silicone breasts, waist cinched like the stem of an hourglass, and legs that appeared airbrushed. Scantily dressed in a tiny one-piece leotard with high-cut legs and a low-cut bodice, the required uniform to brave the relentless heat, I admired Linda, synchronizing with her as we moved through the poses.

I relished the 104-degree heat, the challenge, the movie stars, and the measured compliments and attention Bikram was sending my way. A baptism of sorts, bathing in my sweat, shedding grief, and connecting to a secure space within. It was so difficult that grown men were dropping to their knees in defeat. Not me. I stood for the entire 90-minute sequence. Twenty-six predictable postures, a moving meditation that didn't surprise me. It consoled me. The deep lengthening of the muscles, followed by the stillness in the posture's release, felt like a soothing renewal. I was being introduced to a world of yoga that would become by far the biggest influence of my life. The years I spent as a gymnast were paying off. I heard Dad telling me I could do anything, a profound, motivating imprint that stayed with me for life.

Linda and I would go to Musso Franks on Hollywood Boulevard for a vegetable timbal after yoga class. She was so much fun and so worldly, a make-up artist with Estée Lauder, who wore her long blonde hair in a high ponytail and had a wardrobe full of Pucci dresses. Bikram would usually ask one of us to massage his shoulders and neck while he was lecturing the other students. Sometimes he invited us to the room behind the yoga studio to share a chai tea with him and his brother, Asis.

One night, he suggested that the three of us, not Asis, go out to dinner at Lawry's Steak House. Linda and I were trying to be vegetarians as we thought that is what yoginis are supposed to be. Anyway, we agreed to go out with him. I had never seen Bikram dressed in anything but a tiny black Speedo, so when he came out with white patent leather loafers, tight white polyester bell-bottom pants, and his black shirt unbuttoned down to his navel, I was rather surprised to see this side of him. We hopped into my car (I don't think he had a car yet) and went to dinner at Lawry's. He savored the prime rib, glowing and laughing as he sat proudly between me and Linda—his arms on top of the curved booth enveloping us. We had a little alcohol, and I became aware of where this evening was heading.

Bikram was a virgin, at least that's what he told us, and he said that it would be so perfect to lose his virginity with me and Linda together, and that we should do it tonight after dinner. The evening swept us away from Lawry's and into Linda's bed. Linda's house was an old carriage house, with its bathroom, kitchen, dining room, and bedroom in a single row. It was located behind a mansion in the Hollywood Hills. She was from New Orleans and brought her feminine Southern style with her when she decorated this charming little place. It was filled with beautiful porcelain-painted lamps and art, with fragrant candles burning all around.

Linda and I were feeling a little shy because we weren't used to being with other women, but Bikram had this vision of being with both of us. We were all sort of clumsy and laughing nervously. I think the sheer outrageousness of the situation spurred us on. It was awkward and rather funny, like three youngsters playing doctor with each other. Bikram was like a kid in a candy store. I think we all came away from the experience somewhat embarrassed. It never happened again, and when it came up in conversation with Linda, we laughed and shook our heads. After that, Bikram would sneak a little wink at us in class when nobody was looking. I just rolled my eyes.

I was committed to my yoga practice. In those days, Bikram had not yet been corrupted by Beverly Hills and Hollywood, fancy cars, and women flirting with him. He wasn't yet famous as the "Yogi to the Stars." I felt he truly believed in the power of yoga and that he felt he had a mission to teach as many people as possible.

I spent the next two years doing intense yoga to become a teacher. I had found something to replace gymnastics and, more importantly, something that helped me deal with the loss of my parents. I promised myself I would do yoga for the rest of my life. I felt I had found something so precious and valuable that nobody could take from me.

The structure of the daily class consisted of an opening breathing technique that brought you into the present moment. It was followed by a standing series that stretches the body in all four directions, strengthens all areas, and teaches balance and focus. Then came the floor series, which deepens the flexibility of all the muscles and increases the range of motion in the joints. In the process, all the systems of the body—such as the endocrine, circulatory, and lymphatic systems, along with the internal organs—are positively stimulated and toned. The routine closes with another breathing technique that energizes the body and clears the mind. The final resting pose, lying supine on the floor, was always my favorite. After intense effort, you were rewarded with a blissful state of being unlike any other, far superior to anything that drugs or alcohol could induce. To me, it felt (and still does) like the closest thing to a pure, complete, divine state of well-being.

After diligent practice and dedication, I was able to do each of the 26 postures that comprise the Bikram Yoga Series to perfection in their most advanced form. I could touch my forehead to my toes in a seated forward bend, do complete splits on both sides and in a straddle position, and hold all standing balancing postures in the full expression of the pose with ease. When I walked, I felt like I barely touched the ground. My body was free, flexible, and strong, as close to perfection as it could be. Physically, I had never been so fine-tuned; mentally and emotionally, I felt clear and strong.

After the death of my parents, I had never had any profound professional therapy, except for a few family sessions with my sister, aunt, and uncle, so yoga became my therapy. I felt as though I was sweating out the heartache and pain, leaving it as a wet puddle on the carpet of the yoga studio.

Practicing yoga in the '70s was not common, especially practicing for multiple hours every day. Sometimes I questioned myself, especially when I told someone what I was doing and they reacted by raising their eyebrows and making a strange face. I loved the discipline—it spilled over into other areas of my life—and the sweat-producing heat was purifying. It was better than gymnastics in that it perfected every system of my body. I had never felt so good. Those 26 postures, done the same way every time, allowed me to measure my progress and gave me a sense of accomplishment. It gave me hope. A voice in my head began saying, "You're going to be okay."

Skip Taylor

Skip lived in Laurel Canyon, a neighborhood famous for being home to the rock stars of the '70s. The winding road climbing up from Sunset Boulevard snakes through cozy California bungalows and mini mansions, surrounded by trees and flowers that seem to stay green all year round.

Skip's house was impressive, craftsman style with beautiful woodwork on the floors, walls, and ceilings. A few years later, after Skip had moved out, it burned to the ground. The likely cause was a log rolling out of the fireplace, spreading a flame that nobody noticed. Keith Richards of The Rolling Stones was renting Skip's house. The master bedroom had lead walls, so Keith slept through it and was unharmed.

Skip had slipped me a piece of paper with his phone number on it, along with a phrase like, "I want to be with you." I was sitting by the pool at the apartment I shared with Lisa. It was a surreptitious move because he was on a date with her. Tall and self-assured, he was the type of person who smoothly commanded and controlled the people around him. When he spoke, his beautiful voice made me think he could probably sing. I couldn't resist calling him, and Lisa wasn't interested. She met the Swiss photographer, Olivier, with whom she ended up having a long relationship.

Skip was a big deal in the music industry, working at William Morris Talent Agency. He was a record producer and rock star manager. He managed Fleetwood Mac, Canned Heat, and others.

We rarely went out for dinner on a date. Everything happened at Skip's house. People came and went, and drugs flowed. I was among the musicians and actors at the heart of the music and movie scene of the '70s.

I stood out because everyone else was dressed in jeans and worn-out leather boots. They had layered shag haircuts and smelled of patchouli oil and marijuana. I sported my Vidal Sassoon-designed wedge haircut and my Big Sister platforms from Fred Slatten. I wasn't much into drugs. I was into yoga, which I was only beginning to explore. Thank God. There were lines of cocaine, generously spread throughout Skip's house. Had I not valued my yoga practice as a way to go beyond myself and my circumstances, I could have easily ruined my health and my life.

I somehow became Skip's girl (at least in my mind), which gave me a certain respect at these gatherings. Once everyone left, around three in the morning, we showered together to rid ourselves of the smell of grass and cigarettes, and then made sweet love. I loved the way he wrapped his arms around me and held me. We didn't sleep much. I felt the rapid beat of his heart against my back, driven by the cocaine he had consumed.

He invited me to go to Hawaii with him, along with Fleetwood Mac and their concert-producing entourage. It was the annual Crater Concert there. We took over the first class compartment of the plane, and off we went. I'll never forget my surprise when Skip opened the tray table in front of him and began to blade long lines of cocaine right there during the flight. The flight attendants hurriedly shut the curtains that separated first class and economy. Then they came by and helped themselves. They knew Skip. He created a scene, a party, wherever he went. This party moved to the hotel in Hawaii, and there it never stopped for four days. I walked along the beach with Stevie Nicks. I doubt she remembers me.

Carmen

Carmen Avellaneda was one of the few people in my life who I believe truly loved me. She called me "Chiquita." I was *chiquita*, 5'3" and 107 pounds. She was Fernando's first cousin, also from Acapulco. She came to LA to stay for six months to learn how to cut hair. Fernando taught us at the same time.

Carmen and I made a deal. If she could stay with me for those six months, then I could go to Acapulco and stay with her for six months. It was a perfect arrangement for everyone. Carmen was a bit taller than me. She had a natural elegance and grace about her that I noticed especially when she smoked cigarettes and spoke in her low-pitched voice and Mexican accent. She was well-educated and worldly.

For six months, we went to work every day at Fernando's new salon he opened on Camden Drive. It was a block away from the Vidal Sassoon salon in Beverly Hills. We were diligent students and avid seekers of a good time. Our nocturnal adventures were sometimes hampered when we were exhausted as a result of standing all day watching Fernando's every move . . . aspiring to handle a comb and scissors just like him.

Haircutting is a serious, precise, and challenging skill that involves flipping the comb like a juggler. You first use the wider teeth through the hair, then flip the comb over to use the narrowly placed teeth as a marker for where you are about to actually cut. Fernando preferred a certain type of gray comb. He gave me one, which I still have. He required us to use sharp, Swiss-made, five-inch scissors.

The act of cutting involved quickly moving the thumb up and down in the bottom ring. All the while, you tried not to cut your finger in the process while listening to the many personal details clients felt compelled to delve into once they were in the chair. And of course, you had to make it all look effortless, sort of striking different poses as you cut. I was learning a skill that would serve me for many years to come. A yoga teacher and hair stylist was not what I expected to become when I started out at Loyola with a major in art history.

Carmen was bisexual. I wasn't, but she totally adored me, and I enjoyed her friendship. I was captivated by her sophistication and inspired to be like her. We both had our wedge haircuts and dressed the same way—we were very cool.

I moved out of the apartment with Lisa. She eventually went back to Houston, and we lost contact. I rented a beautiful, spacious apartment on 6th Street near what is now called The Grove. It was white with flowy white curtains and white carpet. We bought futons and brightly colored Japanese covers. That was the only furniture we had. We were never home, so it didn't matter. Carmen danced with the same grace and smoothness as her cousin. Sometimes, Fernando would dance with us at the same time. We were out dancing at My Place or Sergio's Le Club every weekend. We were having an incredible time. He appreciated my enthusiasm for Mexico and my dedication to learning Spanish. Speaking the language allowed me to connect with his family.

In Spanish, there's an expression, *forma de ser*, which means "your way of being." My way of being was solidifying. We were in our natural element, traveling and enjoying every minute of our adventures.

During our time together, Fernando introduced me to Acapulco, a coastal city in Mexico. I instantly felt at home there. The warm tropical breeze embraced me. I sensed something familiar, as though I had previously lived there. A thought arose, *I should live here someday.*

One of Fernando's clients had given him the keys to a cavernous white marble-laden condo on La Costera, the main coastal boulevard. High up with an expansive view of Acapulco Bay, Fernando and I, along with his friend Hiroshi, another famous hairstylist in the making, spent a glorious week together. We toasted our bodies until they were a dark, rich mahogany color with the help of iodine and coconut oil.

Fernando taught me to water ski. We spent time with his humble family, who graciously welcomed us into their home, far removed from the high-rise hotels and glamour. They showed me how to make tortillas, patting and tossing them quickly between the hands until they formed flat, round disks. This was the kick-off trip, launching me into a life in Mexico that would not be with Fernando, as he would eventually leave me for a beautiful Eurasian model named Kay. He broke up with me the moment after he met her. I had never been dumped before, let alone so suddenly. Kay was the one for him. I was not. He remains married to her. They have a family together. I've bumped into them when I go back to Los Angeles. It's always a pleasure but also a sad reminder of how quickly time passes and how much happens after you go your separate ways.

Plank Pose depicts this chapter of my life perfectly. I am holding my own body weight, stable, steady, poised firmly above the ground. My limbs are engaged, my core is strong. I don't rely on anything outside of my body to keep me in place. I do yoga almost every day with an intense heat that causes my body to slowly sweat out the sorrow and grief. I can feel it seep out of my skin, like a purging.

I am gaining confidence, feeling happy again, and laughing. I am exhilarated with my new life in Los Angeles, charged with energy. The sun shines brightly. The Solar Plexus Chakra is the center of vitality, a source of personal power. This vibrant center governs and spreads the energy of fire throughout the system. When balanced, it brings a sense of purpose, a zest for living.

6. Duty

Better a broken promise than none at all.

—Mark Twain

Grasshopper Pose
Chaturanga Dandasana

Chatur means four, anya means limb, danda means staff, and asana means pose. You exhale as you lower your body to hover just above the ground, taking care that you don't fall on your face. You gaze down and support the weight of your entire body on your hands and feet, the only points of contact to the ground. Engage your core abdominal muscles to support your lower back, contract your quadriceps, and squeeze your arms against the torso for added stability.

Root Chakra
Muladhara ~ root support

The Root Chakra is red. It deals with, among other things, security, safety, trust, and stability. It governs survival instincts and is also related to your sense of belonging, being rooted. Located at the base of the spine around the pelvic floor, the root chakra is negatively affected by physical abuse and displacement.

Dimitris

Before I went to Acapulco with Carmen, after Fernando and I broke up, I was briefly married—an arranged marriage—to a Greek man. Athena Vrontikis, daughter of my father's only sister, instigated it. Athena charmed everyone with her slight overbite and a smile that filled half of her face. Her favorite thing to do when she wasn't at home in Salt Lake City, living in her column-flanked Parthenon-esque house, or managing Pete Vrontikis & Son, a well-known appliance store she and her husband owned, was to go on cruises in the Greek Isles. She desired an outlet for fun, a space to shine and showcase her statuesque beauty. On one of those cruises, she met George Rodis and decided he was the perfect husband for her daughter, Sophia. Dimitris, George's first cousin, was perfect for me.

Unbeknownst to me, Athena had made plans for Sophie and me to spend the summer in Greece with the two young Greek men. My plan was to visit Leyla, who had moved back to Tehran, but since Greece was on the way, I agreed to Athena's idea.

Dimitris looked like a Greek god—wavy, tousled hair, a square chiseled jaw, dark, intense eyes, a sculpted nose, and bronze skin. I was drawn to him, and he to me. The only obstacle was the language barrier, but words hardly seemed necessary; we were content just smiling at one another.

Early on, I discovered that Dimitris and I shared a birthday, May 16. *It must be a sign. We're meant to be,* I thought. The summer unfolded between Athens and Epidavros, their family's *chorio* (village). We swam in the sea, feasted on octopus and sea urchins—said to be aphrodisiacs—and it made sense, for life was heavenly.

We packed sandwiches of fresh bread spread with olive oil, layered with luscious local tomatoes and feta cheese, and set off to explore Epidavros. George and Dimitris spearfished, and the local taverna gladly cooked the catch for us. Lunch stretched into night as we lingered over the meal, drinking ouzo, eating slowly, savoring every moment.

Athena told me before our trip that my dad had confided in her before his death that he wished for me to marry a Greek. He told me the same thing in my childhood. I also heard it from my grandmother. I started thinking, "Well, maybe this gorgeous Greek guy is the one I'm meant to marry." If my dad wanted me to marry a Greek, then I had to honor his wishes. Before the summer was over, Dimitris asked me to marry him, and I said, "Yes." I resumed my travels to Tehran to visit Leyla and her husband to absorb the shock of agreeing to get married to a man I knew so little about. The trip was a memorable crescendo of my friendship with Leyla.

When I met Cameron, Leyla, and their family, I didn't dream of visiting Leyla and her husband in Tehran. When they moved back, they invited me to visit, giving me the chance to immerse myself in their culture. Tehran was different back then—bustling, cosmopolitan, and full of possibility. The Shah was in power, and radio stations even offered English lessons, filling the air with voices that mingled Persian with foreign accents.

The homes I visited were lavishly furnished, with handwoven Persian rugs spread across cool marble floors, silver tea services gleaming on low tables, and vibrant artwork lining the walls. The scent of cardamom and saffron rose from the kitchen, where tea and sweets were waiting. Everyone I met dressed fashionably—women in elegant dresses or tailored manteaus, men in sharp suits or bell-bottom trousers with wide collars, looking as though they had stepped out of a European fashion magazine. The city's streets thrummed with Western music, fashionable cafés, and the swirl of tradition and modernity side by side.

Wealthy Persians often flew to Paris to shop, returning with the latest couture fashions. At night, they dressed in style for discos that pulsed with the era's international dance hits. Western culture was being eagerly embraced, and Tehran's educated, sophisticated population seemed intent on living in step with the rest of the world.

Years later, I met the Shah of Iran himself and Farah Diba when they were in exile in Mexico. I was privileged to spend time with Farah. We had memorable conversations on a variety of subjects. She was gracious, kind, and radiantly poised, carrying herself with the quiet dignity of someone once crowned Shahbanu, the first and only Empress of Iran. Despite the grandeur of her past, she busied herself with simple, human tasks—constantly answering letters and correspondence from exiled Iranians who still looked to her as a symbol of hope.

In that short period of time, being in Farah's presence taught me the importance of truly seeing people—looking them in the eye and treating them kindly, even if they were only there for a fleeting service. Imagine her state of mind: she had been forced to flee her beloved country, her husband, the Shah, was dying of kidney cancer, and yet she sat with me the entire afternoon, unhurried, practicing the Farsi Cameron and his family had taught me. Her elegance was not only in her couture or her bearing, but in the way she made you feel as though you mattered.

After my visit, I phoned Cameron's family to share my time with her. They hardly believed it—what an extraordinary opportunity it was to know, even briefly, a woman whose life had once been so public and gilded, yet in exile was defined by loss, resilience, and grace.

After the trip to see Leyla, geography created a natural barrier to our friendship. I crossed paths with Leyla and Cameron in our later years but didn't remain close. I had a surprise run-in with Camron in Vail. Many years went by. He shared with me that their parents had passed. We reminisced and said our goodbyes.

While I was in Tehran, before officially moving back to Salt Lake, Athena was planning two big fat Greek weddings because Sophie decided to marry George. I got married first, on January 11, 1976, in a large ceremony with six bridesmaids standing with me. My wedding colors were cream and dusty rose. I wore Fred Slatten shoes, a fond reminder of my blissful days in LA. The platforms were encrusted with undulating rows of pearls and rhinestones. The wedding took place at the Holy Trinity Greek Orthodox Church. The church I missed. The place where the funeral services for my parents were held.

I could feel Dad's presence there as Dimitris and I stood for the sacred ritual. The priest crowned us with the "*stefana*" (στεφάνι), delicate circles of gold leaves and pearls, connected by a long satin ribbon symbolizing unity. Our best man, George, who was to marry Sophie a few months later, stood as our "*koumbaros*" or best man. We both had a sip of wine from the blessed chalice the priest held. Despite the extravagance and my outward appearance, I felt like crying throughout the ceremony, but not tears of joy. I sensed our marriage wouldn't work. I was standing there to fulfill my father's wishes.

There must have been a thousand people at our wedding reception at the Hotel Utah. The tables were stacked with pillars of Greek pastries—baklava and the traditional wedding cookies dusted with powdered sugar. We had a huge banquet dinner, live bouzoukia music, and a band. I didn't know half of the people there. I had nothing to do with the planning other than picking out my wedding dress and choosing my bridesmaids. Athena orchestrated everything.

I was uneasy the entire day. It got worse when we got back to our hotel room that evening. Dimitris was drunk and began throwing things, yelling in Greek. I took off my shoes. He grabbed one of them and threw it across the room.

We couldn't have a conversation due to the language barrier, but we still managed to argue. I understood little of his anger, only that he was upset none of his family members came to the wedding—they didn't have passports. It might have been him confronting his proud heritage with the realization that his family in Greece was poor, and the situation there was difficult. Our families had pushed us into it. His urging him to marry who they wrongly thought to be a wealthy Greek woman, and mine putting in the effort to honor my father's wishes. I think we both knew we made a mistake. The arrangement wasn't going to work.

The tender moments when we first met in Greece, lying next to each other on the hot pebbly beach, refreshing ourselves in the cool water of the Aegean Sea, receded. The initial mystery was replaced by the reality of displacement and his experience of a snowy winter in an unfamiliar city in the United States.

Dimitris began shouting at me regularly. His rage sprang from nowhere. He began hitting me.

I bought a grand English Tudor house on the poshest street in Salt Lake City and a Mercedes 350 SL with the money from the Boeing settlement. Our relationship was much like how he drove the car—reckless. I was spending the money from the Boeing settlement with nobody advising me on financial matters. Dimitris was uncomfortable with my lavish spending. It collided with his leftist ideology. He was politically active and vociferous about fighting against the evils of capitalism in Greece.

As a child, I observed my father buying new cars, an airplane, and a big house. I guess I was emulating him as I grieved. I lost him before he advised me on financial matters.

Dimitris was a dental technician. He had found a job in Salt Lake City and invited twenty or more of his co-workers to dinner at our home several times per week. Our home turned into a Greek taverna. He prepared at least ten dishes of mezze, including small fried fish, hummus, feta, olives, and more, swimming in Greek olive oil. He missed Greece; we didn't communicate and barely knew each other. After his guests left, in his drunkenness, he hit me or the dog to vent his anger and frustration.

After three months, I had had enough. He went to work one day, and I changed the locks, never letting him back in the house, never to see or speak to him again. I fulfilled my dad's wish but couldn't suffer any more broken lips or bruises. The marriage was annulled. The last I heard, Dimitris passed away, leaving a son and a wife behind. Leaving him, I did everything I could to not look back.

The strength and happiness I found in Los Angeles with my yoga practice held me through this earth-shaking period. As in Chaturanga, Grasshopper Pose, my arms are bent, strained to the max under the pressure to marry Dimitris. I was strong enough to hold my body weight. The dedication to maintaining strength through yoga and the maturity I gained from living on my own in LA sustained me. I'm hovering inches above the Earth, but I am determined. I am a survivor, and I will not let myself collapse.

Trauma impacts the Root chakra, holding the energy from physical abuse or displacement. I was experiencing both. I didn't belong in Salt Lake City anymore. Being back there, I sensed a judgmental gaze from people, especially those in the Greek community who knew I had lost my parents. I was a curiosity to them, an orphan who had inherited a lot of money. The news of my parents' dramatic death was on the front page of *The Salt Lake Tribune*, complete with a photo of the plane trailing smoke, about to crash into Mt. Fuji. News of the crash made it into *Life Magazine*. The publicity and images of the dead bodies of the crash stuck with me—victims lined up with the remnants of the plane in the background. My dad was president of the Holy Trinity Greek Orthodox Church, where I married Dimitris. Everybody knew Dad, and everything felt like a reminder of my grief. In my early adulthood, I was reliving the tragedy that struck when I was twelve, and the new trauma of physical abuse was adding to my longing for my parents.

The instincts of fight, flight, or freeze emanate from the survival center that is the Root chakra. This part of me was being activated. I couldn't fight back and hit Dimitris in the face. If I froze and stayed in an abusive marriage, I would be stuck in a city where I didn't want to live and a life that wasn't meant for me. I took flight and left quickly before it was too late.

7. Jetset

Too much of a good thing can be wonderful.

—Mae West

Upward Facing Dog
Urdhva Mukha Svanasana

You push yourself away from the floor, lifting your chest forward and upward, supporting your weight on the palms of your hands and the tops of your feet. The rest of the body does not touch the floor. Press your shoulders down, lift your chest, and expand it fully, proudly, opening your heart. Gaze straight ahead or upward as long as you don't strain your neck. In this powerful backbend, every muscle along the backside of the body is engaged and strengthened.

Throat Chakra
Vishuddha ~ especially pure

The Blue Throat Chakra is associated with truth, purification, sound, and laughter. It's a gateway to our creative potential, empowering self-expression through artistic endeavors. It corresponds to the neck and surrounding area.

The Jet-Setting, Disco-Dancing Hair Stylists in Acapulco

A year after Fernando and I broke up, after I bawled my eyes out and grieved our days doing hair shows and jaunting around Los Angeles, I returned to Acapulco. I never forgot the feeling of home I had there. Going back, I was filled with excitement—happy to keep the promise I had made to myself to live there one day.

After finishing hairstylist training, Carmen wanted to go back to her home in Acapulco. I went with her. That was our original arrangement. On our way, we stopped in Mexico City for a few months, where we worked at a hair salon called Joss in La Zona Rosa. We met many people and enjoyed our time there, but Carmen missed her family.

In Acapulco, she lived with her elderly parents. They immigrated from Spain many years earlier and settled in an upper-middle-class neighborhood in the hills above the bustle of La Costera, where the tourists filled the hotels and restaurants. Her parents were formal, reserved, and private. Her mother was obsessed with preserving her face, incessantly applying creams and massaging her face upwards. She never slept in any position except on her back. She placed a pillow on each side of her head to avoid wrinkles on her face.

Carmen and I occupied the top floor of their house, coming and going as we pleased. It was a good thing her parents didn't wait up for us. Most of the time, we didn't come home until two or three in the morning. There were big, lavish, occasionally themed parties. Carmen knew everyone, so we were invited to every event. Those were the disco days at Armando's Le Club and Baby'O.

But wait, we were hairstylists now, trained by the famous Fernando Romero, artistic director of Vidal Sassoon! We decided to open a hair salon to show off our skills. While lounging next to the chic swimming pool at the Villa Vera Club, cultivating our tans, Carmen said, "Let's call it Copacabana Hair!" I loved the name. It sounded like a party. We found the perfect *locale*, a commercial space right on La Costera behind the hotel El Cano with a view of the Acapulco Bay.

Around that time, we met Hector Von Hoffmeister, a talented Brazilian interior designer in Mexico City. Hector draped the entire space of our new salon with green and white sailcloth, even the ceiling. He pleated and padded the fabric in a myriad of clever, tasteful ways and placed circular, rectangular, and square mirrors everywhere. The effect was dazzling. We hosted a grand opening and dressed in gorgeous silk gowns. The press came and wrote an article about Copacabana Hair.

During high season, November to May, we worked a few hours a day, then readied ourselves to go to the glitzy parties and disco nights that were at their peak during these years. International visitors from Europe and South America came to be part of the happenings. Like LA, Acapulco was an epicenter of dance and fashion. We kept up with the scene.

Most days, our schedule went like this: wake up at 8:00 a.m., go to Lagunilla, and water ski. Afterwards, devour scrumptious huevos rancheros with black beans and freshly squeezed orange juice. Then we'd go home, shower, get dressed, go to our salon, do two or three haircuts, style our own hair, and go home again. While Carmen took a siesta, I rolled out my mat on the cool talavera ceramic floor to practice yoga. I did the same routine, the original 26 postures I had learned from Bikram. It gave me stillness between festivities.

Carmen knew a local tailor, and we brought him photos from *Vogue* of the clothing we wanted copied so we could be dressed in the latest fashion. I even brought a few beautiful pieces from stores like Norma Kamali in Beverly Hills for him to replicate. Our attire had to be danceable, dreamy, stylish, and fitted to perfection.

One of the most unforgettable designs was a Norma Kamali creation—a unique one-piece silk dress. It was a process to put on: a long swath of fabric stitched all around. You begin by holding one end across the bust, tying it at the middle of the back, then bringing the remaining fabric down the front of the body, between the legs, and letting it billow to the knees before tying it at the waist from back to front. It felt like an outfit the actress Barbara Eden wore in *I Dream of Jeannie*. The tailor made it for us in every color.

By appearances, Carmen and I were a huge success. The truth was we were booking clients and gaining attention, but the books reflected moderate revenue, outshined by the fun we were having partying and immersing ourselves in the social scene. We didn't have a waiting list. A consistent flow of clients, yes, but the primary use of the salon was in getting ourselves ready to go out.

We were lean, tan, and sculpted from water skiing and yoga, doing everything possible to look our best—just as everyone around us did. Hours went into shaping our long nails into perfect ovals, painting them a new color each week to match our slightly risqué attire. Our toes, buffed and polished, peeked from strappy Italian sandals—high enough to be glamorous, yet still made for dancing.

Carmen insisted on ice-cold eye douches to brighten our gaze, while our facials were made from a kitchen blend of egg whites and honey, smoothed from forehead to décolleté. Freshly trimmed haircuts, glossy and precise, completed the look.

On weekends, the places to be were the Villa Vera club or Carlos'n Charlie's beach club. There we strutted around in our tiny bikinis and lounged about playing backgammon. We carried a handmade Aries leather backgammon set with us in case someone wanted to play. I was having the most amazing time, taking it all in, getting chicer by the day.

Once in a while, we got together with Carmen's guy cousin. I kind of liked him, but nothing came of it. He was about my age, cute and boyish. We drove with him to a hidden beach and smoked grass known only by the locals, a strain called Peliroja or red hair. Our days were spent eating fresh seafood like huachinango a la veracruzana with olives, peppers, garlic, tomatoes, and shrimp ceviché. We washed it down with cold Corona beer laced with lime juice.

As I am writing this today, I realize it's May 8, Carmen's birthday. What a strange coincidence. I wish I could call her, wish her happy birthday, and let her know how much I appreciated her kindness and generosity. If I could talk to her now, I would thank her for imparting her elegance to me. Our time together influenced my later years for the better. She died at 52 in a hospital in Acapulco from complications associated with peritonitis. When she passed, she lived in Connecticut with an older man who was involved in the art world. That's all I knew of her. We weren't in touch after I left Mexico.

Acapulco in the '70s felt like a *pueblo* if you ventured off of La Costera. Many roads were unpaved. The locals lived in their little colonias, where you found the *tortillerías* and tiny stores, or *almacenes*, selling *chicles*, gooey sweets made from tamarind, *mazapán*, and cigarettes. Acapulco was primitive, but there were many conveniences—a tailor, a shoe repair shop, and an auto mechanic. Skilled craftsmen were available to build and repair just about anything. Their artistry was apparent in the carefully constructed walls around town, chiseled from local rocks.

The local Acapulcanos and the visiting jet-setters were breathing the same air and experiencing the same weather but were worlds apart. Some of the people I met were the likes of Harold Robbins, the wildly popular novelist whose lurid, best-selling books about sex and power mirrored the excesses he seemed to live by. He wanted Carmen and me to have a foursome with him and his wife, Grace. There was no chance of that—we thought they were old and perverse.

Another Grace, Grace Jones, performed regularly in Acapulco in front of a small audience in a club. Carmen and I thought she was fabulous. We attended two of her shows back to back. She writhed on the stage, microphone in hand, singing in her velvety, androgynous voice, dressed in a leopard bodysuit with sculpted, shiny short hair. She changed into another outfit as wild, bold, and outrageous for the second show.

Teddy Stauffer, a Swiss musician, was the biggest playboy of the era. Word spread (a rumor he started) that he would leave his estate to whomever he was making love to at the time of his death. Many women went to bed with him, hoping they would be the one to give him a heart attack. This went on for years. What a perfect scheme he had devised.

Tony Starr was the real star of Acapulco. She was from New York, and she was striking with big honey-colored hair, curves, and an angelic face. Her eyes sparkled when she looked at you. She held court wherever she was, never without a cigarette in her delicate, manicured hand. The Mexican entrepreneur, Armando Sotres, fell in love with her. They had two girls, Kali and then Erika, who later changed her name and became a famous actress known today in Mexico as Issabela Camil.

Armando had one of the first successful discotecas in Acapulco called Armando's Le Club in the Taj Mahal. The locale had grand latticed archways and thick white columns surrounded by a vast swimming pool. Day or night, it dazzled.

Tony left Armando for Roberto Trouyet, whose family was extremely wealthy. Roberto's family developed the beautiful hilltop resort called Las Brisas, perched on forty acres looking out on the Acapulco Bay. From there, one could spot one of the many pink and white Jeeps transporting the guests throughout the resort.

Roberto had an enormous mansion there and, with Tony, hosted movie stars and jet-setting partiers from around the world. They came on their yachts and private planes to see and be seen, imbibe, dance, and sunbathe. The ambiance was carefree and fun, fueled by alcohol and drugs. An air of sophistication and decadence permeated every gathering—a constant buzz of excitement. I attended lavish parties, one with an Egyptian theme. The guests wore elaborate costumes. For Tony's grand entrance, she dressed as Cleopatra. Four men carried her above their heads on a large platform, upon which she reclined. Drugs and alcohol flowed. Much was going on behind closed doors, but I didn't ask questions.

While I was having a fabulous time in the year I was there, a growing uneasiness began welling up inside of me. After the novelty wore off, I looked closely at the scene around me. The people who lived this lifestyle looked empty when they weren't drinking or relishing in the allure of the parties. They appeared deflated. In the daylight, their faces were red and puffy, aged. Years of alcohol and drugs left deep lines and creases and dulled their leathery tan skin.

I didn't want to end up like the perennial party-goers of Acapulco. I told Carmen it was time for me to figure out my next move. It would have been easy to stay and get sucked back into the scene. My yoga practice brought me back to center, to my trustworthy inner voice. That inner voice told me this lifestyle was not my destiny. My practice allowed me to have a taste, a glimpse of this feral, crazy time in Acapulco without being seduced by it.

I had experienced the true joy of regular yoga practice and a healthy lifestyle. This rectifying habit kept me straight my whole life. I knew how to manage my innate tendencies. Even my astrological profile lined up with what I already sensed. I am a Taurus with my moon in Scorpio, and that gives me the tendency to indulge in the sensual things of life . . . sex, delicious food, soft skin and sumptuous fabrics, romantic, flirtatious people, and beauty. I know if it weren't for yoga, I would indulge in the lavishness offered to me in Acapulco to an extreme degree.

In this chapter of my life, I experienced freedom of self-expression through the creation of my first business, Copacabana Hair. I attended many parties, met many people, and danced endlessly at famous discos.

I mingled with the wealthy aristocrats, the jet-setters of the world, observing them, learning how to be sophisticated and charming with manners and grace.

In the yoga posture Upward Facing Dog, Urdhva Mukha Svanasana, the chest proudly thrusts forward, lifting and rising. The support of the torso is derived from the arms and upper body and the muscles throughout the backside of the body, especially the muscles that uphold the spine in an arched hyper-extended position. As in this posture, when I was bending backwards, about to fall back, I found power to catch and sustain me. After the painful experience at the hands of an abusive man, I rose and opened my heart to bliss and laughter again. I learned to be independent long ago. I was standing firm on my own, as one does in this pose, looking ahead with confidence.

The throat chakra loves laughter, freedom of expression, sound, and authenticity. I was free at this time of my life, giggling, singing at the top of my lungs as I danced. I was becoming fluent in another language, expressing myself through a new filter that somehow felt familiar and natural. The Spanish language intrigued me the first time I heard it. Now I was speaking it—able to translate my feelings, needs, and wants using new words.

8. Initiations

Awakening is not changing who you are, but discarding who you are not.

—Deepak Chopra

Downward Facing Dog
Adho Mukha Svanasana

You place your hands shoulder distance apart, spreading your fingers and pressing firmly against the ground. Visualize creating one straight line of energy from the hands to the buttocks and another from the buttocks to the heels. Tilt the sacrum so the tail-bone points to the sky while attempting to press the heels down towards the ground. When doing this posture, you are basically upside down, gazing at yourself while fresh blood is sent rushing to the head. In the Sun Salutation, it marks another major transition where you go from facing out to facing in. It feels restorative as it requires less energy to maintain than the previous postures, even though you are still stretching and strengthening many areas of the body.

Third Eye Chakra
ajna ~ to perceive

The color of this chakra is indigo. It governs multiple aspects of a person's life, similar to the chakras, and sometimes co-governs with other chakras. Self-realization, clarity, clairvoyance, and intuition are a few of them. It allows you to see beyond the physical realm and into higher levels of consciousness, gifting spiritual awareness. It is located in the center of the forehead.

From Acapulco to Polanco

Carmen stayed in Acapulco. I didn't want to return to the US. I had my Mexican working visa and continued perfecting my Spanish. I left Acapulco and everyone there behind for Mexico City. When I arrived, I secured a position at one of the affiliate hair salons owned by Joss called Joss/Jose Luis. Carmen and I had previously worked for Joss, but not at that location.

The salon was in a converted grand mansion built in the 1930s. It was a full-service salon with a make-up artist, chef, and talented hair stylists, decorated by Hector Von Hoffmeister, who had done

Copacabana Hair. This time, he draped lush brown velvet fabric everywhere, tufted, quilted, and punctuated by mirrors of many shapes and sizes.

Everyone was done up at Joss/Jose Luis, myself included. I wore high heels when cutting hair. The clients were wealthy women from the reigning families in Mexico City, whose photos filled the social columns in the newspapers and magazines. My clients filled me in on the gossip, sitting in the chair, telling me about their social lives and personal dramas. Even though I wasn't of their social class, they invited me to swanky cocktail and dinner parties. They liked that I was young, foreign, and somewhat of a curiosity.

Living in Polanco, the Beverly Hills of Mexico, I was situated among the ultra-sophisticated crowd. The neighborhood was residential, with a European chocolate shop a few doors from the salon and a delicious Spanish tapas bar around the corner on Campos Eliseos. Nearby was Polancito (little Polanco), where you'd find an open-air market, butcher shop, coffee shops, and *pequeñas tiendas*, small stores, for everyday needs. It was the perfect place for me.

My First Yoga Studio

Bikram gave me permission to open a branch of his organization, the *Yoga College of India*, which was the name of the school he founded to spread his style of yoga. He liked the idea of expanding his teachings outside of LA. I found a spacious one-bedroom apartment on a street called Socrates and converted the living room into a yoga studio. It had a large glass sliding door and floor-to-ceiling windows that allowed for ample natural light. I used masking tape I applied to the entire width of the doors, leaving an inch in between strips to give the illusion of shades. I installed mirrors and fresh carpet before welcoming my first students.

The word spread about my yoga classes throughout the hair salon, and I organized a grand opening that made the social section of the major Mexico City newspaper. The write-up featured photos of the attendees dressed in saris and me demonstrating yoga postures.

People came to the grand opening out of curiosity. They never heard of a yoga studio. We gathered, sipping steaming cups of chai tea and nibbling on Indian pastries prepared by one of the guests. The air was filled with the intoxicating aroma of cardamom, cinnamon, and ginger—warm spices that wrapped around us with the grounding energy of a well-rooted asana. It was something novel, and the who's who of Mexico City wanted to be a part of it.

I taught one morning class and one evening class and cut hair at the salon in between. The studio flourished for a year. When the lease on my apartment came up for renewal, the landlord decided he didn't want a yoga studio in his building. I closed the studio and relocated.

Linda, my friend with whom I practiced Bikram yoga in Los Angeles, moved to Mexico City after discovering the many opportunities for make-up artists doing fashion shows and television. We found a wonderful little house to rent in Las Lomas on Cerrado de Sierra Vertientes, close to Polanco, a short commute to Joss/Jose Luis Salon.

Shaktipat

Carol Huffstickler was a tall, well-dressed blonde woman from Texas who also happened to be an astrologer and psychic. One of my clients introduced us. Carol had an impressive resume, serving as a consultant on government-level projects, investigating ships and aircraft that disappeared when they crossed into the Bermuda Triangle. Her psychic abilities proved valuable in high-level investigations and unsolved mysteries.

She had come to Mexico City to give readings. I felt compelled to sign up. Carol started the session by placing a small photo of her guru, Baba Muktananda, on the table. She explained he was an enlightened, perfected being and a spiritual master in the tradition of Siddha yoga. We found a candle, lit it, and she began the reading.

"When is your birthday?" she asked me.

"May 16."

"You share a birthday with Baba," she said.

I stared at the photo of him, allured and amused, we were born on the same day. Me and this smiling man from India, wearing an orange knitted cap and a red dot on his forehead, had something in common.

"You are about to embark on an intense spiritual journey," she told me.

"I've been practicing yoga for several years now," I explained, thinking I was on the journey she spoke of.

"Yoga has prepared you for what's coming next," she said.

My astrological chart indicated I was a teacher of yoga or dance or something involving the physical body. She described my personality traits and key moments in my life, but nothing surprised me more than when she said, "You experienced the death of one or both of your parents around the age of twelve."

She had my attention. I had to know more about her guru. "Can I meet Baba?" I asked. Carol suggested I visit one of his centers. "There is one in LA, and although he might not be there, you can find his books and attend a meditation and chanting session there."

I felt compelled to take her suggestion and planned a short weekend trip to Los Angeles.

I returned to Mexico City with a few of Baba's books I had bought at Muktananda's Siddha Yoga Meditation Center and began reading *A Play of Consciousness* one evening after work—Baba's autobiography. To my uninitiated surprise, the book transmitted *shaktipat*, the divine energy of awakening. The yogic texts describe shaktipat as an initiation that activates an inner unfolding of awareness that leads to progressively higher states of consciousness. Spiritual awakening, or the awakening of the latent kundalini energy, happens in several ways. Shaktipat can be transmitted by reading a book that is infused with divine energy, written by an enlightened being. It can come from a glance, a touch, or being in the presence of such a being.

After a few chapters into the book, I sensed a dreamy wave wash over my body, synonymous with the effect of anesthesia entering your body. I was transported into a trancelike spiritual state, unlike anything I had ever experienced—crying and laughing, moving through a wide spectrum of emotions. My body spontaneously writhed, shook, and assumed strange positions. Between these episodes, I continued to read the book, clinging to every word. I became freezing cold and shook with chills. Minutes later, I was sweating as though I had a fever. This went on throughout the night. I didn't know what was happening, but somehow I wasn't afraid. I had a sense I was watching it unfold from a distant place, like a remote observer.

By morning, I felt calm, in a serene, meditative state. I had experienced a spiritual awakening that propelled me into the world of Siddha Yoga. Under the aegis of this international organization, there were ashrams where seekers stayed for extended periods, as well as centers open for day or evening visits. These gathering places were devoted to ancient teachings rooted in Kashmir Shaivism and Hinduism.

Over the next two decades, I spent months at a time in ashrams across several locations. There, I meditated, chanted, studied, learned to play the tamboura, and recited the *Guru Gita* and *Rudram*. But first, I had to meet Baba Muktananda—who, as fate had it, was coming to Miami.

Rosa Schultz

I discovered a small Siddha Yoga center near me in Mexico City. Rosa Schultz was a regular attendee at the morning meditations and chants and the evening programs that featured lectures and more chanting.

Most days, I drove my little Renault 5, a stick of Nag Champa incense burning on the dashboard, to this large house/spiritual center in colonial Anzures next to Polanco. Rosa was a silver-haired vixen old enough to be my mother. She had bright blue eyes and pearl-white teeth. Rosa had an innate sense of style, accessorized and polished. We became friends and traveled together to meet Baba.

In Siddha Yoga, it is customary to surrender your addictions to the guru to relieve yourself of burdens. I didn't know that for Rosa, it meant bringing a large plastic baggie filled with marijuana and bottles of liquor—tequila, vodka, and rum—on the flight. She pulled everything out of her carry-on to show me en route to Miami.

Shocked, I didn't think we would make it to the ashram together. I wanted no part of it. "Rosa, when we step off this plane, you are going through customs on your own. I am going to Miami for spiritual enlightenment, not to be arrested!"

She got through customs without issue, stuffed the grass into her bra, and flirted her way through. This was the beginning of our two-month stay in Miami at a motel ashram.

Baba Muktananda

I'll never forget the first time I saw Baba Muktananda in person. I anticipated this moment for six months. It began with the astrological reading with Carol, followed by my travels to LA to buy the books and visit the Siddha Yoga Center. Then I received shaktipat, the transmission of spiritual energy, when I read his autobiography.

When I finally saw Baba in person, the experience met my highest expectations. If you were lucky, you'd get a glimpse of him during the day on the grounds of the ashram, perhaps a chance encounter in the hallway as he walked with his entourage. But in the evening, everyone got to see him.

Darshan is the opportunity to see an enlightened or holy person. In Hinduism, it is highly auspicious. The evening programs were eagerly awaited, and a palpable air of excitement permeated the room. Everyone dressed up. We chanted and listened to heartfelt stories told by swamis dressed in their orange robes. We looked forward to the chance to line up and take our turn to kneel in front of Baba.

He sat there on the dais, one hand holding a large swath of peacock feathers infused with essential oils that he bopped on everyone's head. He greeted each person with affection, one by one, looking directly into our eyes. When my eyes met his, his gaze entered my eyes and went directly to my heart. I felt a shot of warmth and tender love in that moment. It was blissful. When I think about it so many years later, the feeling still touches my soul.

Discipline-Living in an Ashram

Living in an ashram is an extraordinary experience. People say you burn through your karma at a faster pace. Your deepest fears rise to the surface, forcing you to confront and release them. The qualities you most abhor might show up in the very person who becomes your roommate.

Rosa and I became that for each other. We fought and argued, vowing never to see each other again, then cried and made up. Everything she did bugged me, and I know she felt the same about me. She kept me up with her nightmares and night sweats (she was going through menopause), showing complete disregard for my loss of sleep. I was impatient with her because she was always convinced she had lost something, constantly rummaging through her many little bags of stuff. It drove me crazy.

I'm not sure how karma works, and I have come to believe it is impossible to understand. But I can tell you that, time after time, while living in the ashram, I found myself in situations that tested my patience and forced me to stop and observe my reactions. Every encounter was magnified and exaggerated. This manifested in something as simple as being seated next to someone who sniffled constantly through morning meditation, disrupting the noble quest to find bliss. Or someone next to me singing loudly, completely off-key, during a chant, thus ruining my existential experience.

Being at an ashram is a constant play of staying focused on the divine while navigating the interruptions and distractions that inevitably arise. As I look back, I learned invaluable lessons that taught me patience and how to observe my reactions instead of identifying with them. I learned that life can't be perfect, even when living in an ashram, nor is it meant to be, because without challenges, you cease to grow. I learned to embrace whatever comes my way, observe it, and use it as an opportunity to evolve.

The daily schedule at the Miami ashram began with a 4 a.m. group meditation in a large, dark, freezing room. Rosa and I set our alarms early, making sure we had enough time to do our makeup—there was fashion, even in an ashram. We painted a red bindi in the center of our foreheads to aid in opening the third eye and lined our other two eyes with dark kohl pencil. Our outfits were comfortable yet stylish: long skirts paired with sweaters and, of course, a shawl or silk scarf. Every woman wore some variation of this look. It was a far cry from the days in Acapulco, but I welcomed the change.

After we finished getting ready, we hurriedly gathered our wool meditation blankets along with the Guru Gita and Rudram books for the chanting sessions that ensued. Then we dashed off to arrive before the doors closed. One must be on time for everything at an ashram. Timeliness was part of the discipline, the motive being that it helped us live better in our everyday lives.

In meditation, there were two suggested mantras: "Om Namah Shivaya," which means "I honor my inner self," or "Ham Sa," which can be reversed to "So Ham," a mantra representing the sound of the breath. All three are used in tune with the breath's rhythm.

Some days, I meditated for the entire hour and stayed focused on the mantra. Others, unexpected autogenous thoughts surfaced out of nowhere. My body cooperated, having maintained an unbreakable hatha yoga practice. Those years of doing Bikram yoga enabled me to sustain a full or half lotus posture for long periods of time. I was rarely distracted when a part of my body went numb or became achy. This proved to be advantageous for meditating and chanting.

I held my spine upright, allowing the prana—the life force—to flow freely through the energy channels of my etheric body. The etheric body, in simple terms, receives this life force and transmits it to the physical body, sustaining it through the circulation of blood and the workings of the endocrine and nervous systems.

Occasionally, a kriya arises in my body during meditation. The first time it happened was during this stay at the ashram. A kriya is an involuntary movement that seems to emerge from nowhere. It is considered a purifying process and is not meant to be given much attention. In my case, my torso shudders and rotates rapidly from side to side.

Some practitioners form hand mudras, their fingers and palms moving into shapes like those seen in images of Hindu deities. At first, when I witnessed this in fellow meditators, I assumed it was contrived—until I experienced a kriya myself. It still happens to me, though only during extended, profound meditations such as those uniquely possible in an ashram setting.

Meditation provokes latent sadness to well up from deep within. This serves as a release of unresolved experiences. Conversely, you may feel pure joy and elation springing from the heart. Both can produce tears. Some people laugh, others scream. The meditation room at the ashram held fifty to sixty people, all of whom were away from home, feeling the intensity and demands of the rigorous daily routine. Some days, I laughed to myself, thinking it sounded like a zoo. Every meditation session was a unique experience in which I had to trust the process and accept that whatever was happening was appropriate on my quest for self-realization. The same held true for everyone else.

After meditation, we took a short break before returning to the lotus position to chant the *Guru Gita* for an hour. This beautiful devotional chant carries a simple melody but intricate wording, as it is sung in Sanskrit. Divided into three sections and comprising 182 verses, the *Guru Gita* praises the virtues of the guru, which I interpret as one's own inner self.

The chant is so intricate that if your focus drifts, it can be difficult to find your place again, a challenge that trains the mind in the art of one-pointedness. Imagine being guided by the resonant tones of the tanpura and harmonium with the fragrance of incense drifting through the room. Then add the joy of merging your voice with fifty others, chanting as one. The effect is truly intoxicating.

After chanting the Guru Gita, we had nectar for the soul in the form of breakfast. The savory sour soup served in the Siddha Yoga ashrams and centers is absolutely delicious, a comforting warm dish to wake up your tummy. Dubbed "enlightenment soup," it contains millet, onion, coconut, tomato, ginger, dates, cilantro, and hot chile pepper as well as fragrant spices and seeds such as cumin, cayenne, coriander, and fenugreek. The people who participate in the making of the soup chant or internally recite the mantra the entire time they are preparing it. The energy of that act is truly palpable. A cup of chai, a bathroom stop, and on to the next chant . . . one and a half hours sitting still to chant the Rudram.

Shri Rudram is a Vedic chant paying homage to Rudra, an aspect of Shiva, the yogi god of transformation and stillness. Much more complicated and faster-paced than the Guru Gita, it requires even more focus and is an amazing tool for sharpening the mind. It's divided into two parts, the first being Namakam, in which the devotee invokes the graceful and benevolent aspect of Shiva and asks to be forgiven for sins. In the second part, called Chamakam, one asks for the fulfillment of wishes. This is a simplistic explanation. It is far more complex. The experience of chanting Rudram is powerful and exceptionally challenging.

Next on the daily schedule was hatha yoga, followed by some form of work. Referred to as *seva* in Sanskrit, this is the practical labor needed to run an ashram. Everyone had to contribute: it could be cleaning the public toilets, preparing food, or vacuuming the meditation hall. Whatever task you were assigned, the idea was to do it while internally reciting the mantra *"Om Namah Shivaya"*—which means *"I bow to Shiva,"* or more broadly, *"I honor the divine within"*—the entire time.

I came to love the routine of living at the ashram. Bikram yoga prepared me in myriad ways, on many levels, purifying, clearing the energy channels of my etheric body, fine-tuning the systems of my physical body, and ingraining discipline overall. Now, I felt I was taking my existence to the next level. The daily activities, meditation, chanting, mentally reciting the mantra throughout every mundane task, and the life lessons I learned through the stories told in the evening programs with Baba Muktananda were deepening my sadhana, or spiritual practice, in a remarkable way. They were enabling me to feel a deeper connection to my authentic inner being.

The chanting was healing my childhood wounds from the loss of my parents. I felt my heart opening. I was honing not just my body but my mind as well, developing tools to harness my emotions and thoughts instead of being a slave to them. Learning to embrace what happened to me gave me a sense of control over my life. The skills I was acquiring would help me handle whatever difficulties awaited me.

After living in the ashram for a couple of months, it was time to leave, say goodbye to Rosa, and return to Mexico City and my work. My time with her was transformative. We see parts of ourselves that need healing in our struggles with others.

Rosa taught me patience.

She was like my mother, giving me sound advice. Even though we had our moments, most of the time we got along and liked each other's company.

I saw a bit of myself in her in that she was adventurous and seductive; she loved men, and they loved her. She was strong-willed, and so am I. Rosa and I remained in touch and visited one another over the years until she passed away fifteen years ago.

One afternoon, after returning to Mexico City from the ashram, I was sitting in the lobby of Joss/Jose Luis. Jean, the French receptionist, sat behind the desk, a thin stream of smoke curling from his pungent Gitanes cigarette. He glanced at me, inquiring, "What're you doing back here?"

The question caught me off guard. I lurched inward, scrambling for an answer. It was one of those unexpected aha moments people often describe—but I remained silent.

What was I doing alone in Mexico City? I had no other place to go. Yes, Linda and I had a nice house, but she was busy with her work and her new boyfriend. Change felt necessary. Then, the idea of settling, marrying, and forming a family took hold.

Michel

I first met Michel long before my conversation with Jean, before I ever thought of having children. Fernando had broken up with me, and I was still mourning the relationship. I bumped into Michel on the street in front of Fernando's salon. I was still working there. We started talking. Michel invited me to dinner, but I was apprehensive about getting involved with another man. The only man I had truly loved left me so abruptly. I agreed to go to dinner and surprised Michel by bringing a few friends, which he wasn't too happy about. We had a wonderful evening at Carlos 'n Charlie's on the Sunset Strip, but the meeting didn't turn into anything more. A few months later, I ran into him again at a party in Acapulco. I had a gut feeling I was supposed to be with him.

Michel wore an incessant grin filled with a mouth full of flawless enamel. He had smooth, caramel-colored skin and a compact, nicely built body, and he was well read and cultured. He gave me his phone number, but I didn't call him until a couple of years later, after Jean asked me why I was in Mexico City. I thought Michel could be the one with whom I would settle down and have a family.

We started dating and going to Cuernavaca on the weekends with his mother, Maka. In spite of her tepid reception of me, Michel asked me to move in with him just a few months later. I agreed to do so even though I was afraid to risk giving myself to another man after Fernando. My desire to have a child was growing stronger. Michel fit the profile of a good father.

His family didn't have money, but they had culture and education. My family was not involved in the arts, and I always wished I had that growing up. Michel could give my child what I always wanted. He made me laugh. I was comforted by his subtlety and kindness.

Michel had a nice two-bedroom apartment on Rio Danubio in Mexico City near the golden towering monument of El Ángel, also known as the Monumento a la Independencia. It didn't take long for me to become pregnant. We settled into a comfortable routine—happy, not passionately or crazy in love, but it worked. A few months before our son, Demian, was born, we decided to get married.

Maka

Interesting is a pale word when it comes to describing Maka.

The first time I met her, Michel came to pick me up. He invited me to spend the weekend in Cuernavaca. I walked out of my house and headed toward the car to take the front seat next to Michel, only to find Maka already sitting where I thought I'd be, as Michel's date. Wrong.

She looked at me and sternly motioned to the back seat with her thumb, indicating that was where I was going to sit. Okay, well, whatever. I hopped into the back seat. She barely acknowledged me during the entire one and a half hour drive to Cuernavaca. I realized then that this was not going to be easy, and I was right. Maka dominated my soon-to-be husband. They talked for an hour on the phone every evening without exception. She summoned him, and he always answered the call.

Maka spoke eight languages. She was erudite and worldly—a well-regarded author, painter, and intellectual born in Paris in 1925. She was the only daughter of the Russian count Vladimir Czernichew, who, while exiled in Paris, married Rosa Maria Dorantes, a young girl from Mexico studying in Paris. They named her Maria Magdalena Czernichew Dorantes, later using the name Maka. Her mother and father dropped her off at a boarding school in Paris when she was three. She spent most of her youth there while her parents travelled and partied. As a young woman, she modeled for *Vogue*. Some say that later, during World War II, she was an agent for the Resistance.

It was easy to see how she could have seduced or cajoled anyone into doing what she wanted. Her presence was powerful. A great figure and model-esque, symmetrical face, she could wear anything or cut her hair in any style and always look amazing. During subsequent trips to Cuernavaca with her, we drove to her home in the La Condesa neighborhood to pick her up.

Each time she stepped out of her front door, it took me a minute to recognize her. Sometimes she chopped off her hair and colored it henna red. The next week she was blonde. Her style of dressing was eccentric bohemian. She heaped on loads of chunky jewelry, amber necklaces, silver antique bracelets, and topped it off with a turban wrapped around her head. One time, she appeared in a white gauzy dress, no make-up or jewelry, taking on the persona of a renunciate living in a purified state of being, speaking softly and calmly. You never knew what to expect from her. She was brilliant and creative and fearless.

I felt small under Maka's big, brown-eyed gaze. Her level of intelligence scared me. Her conversations, mostly one-sided, were about literary figures, historical events, or the latest play being produced in Mexico by her closest friends. Among her intimate, talented circle was artist Juan Soriano, known for his monumental sculptures, the writer Gabriel Garcia Marquez, the brilliant novelist and art critic Juan Garcia Ponce, and her dear friend and fellow painter Cordelia Urueta. She and Cordelia must have had so much in common as artists working with color and abstraction. Cordelia also lived in Paris in the '30s and was regarded as an intellectual.

John Huston, the notable American filmmaker, was Maka's best friend and lover. She was his muse. I had the chance to meet John when he was in Cuernavaca filming *Under the Volcano*. Michel and I had lunches and dinners with him and Maka. He was on oxygen, suffering from emphysema, but still able to hold court in his grand, charismatic manner.

I saw why he and Maka were close. They both had an enormous presence. I was in awe of them, afraid to say anything for fear of sounding like an idiot. I was observing and learning. It made me realize how much I had to learn and how different my background was in comparison. I don't think I ever saw my father or mother reading classic literature. The gaps in my education were starting to gnaw at me. I was driven to make use of the opportunity to listen closely to the conversations around me.

Besides John Huston, Maka had many other influential, high-profile creative men in her life, such as the writer Octavio Paz and the actor Anthony Quinn. Her attitude towards me and the look on her face on the rare occasions when she addressed me were of mild disdain. She had figured out I was not *culta*, or cultured, at least nowhere near her level. When she had guests come for lunch in Cuernavaca, I struggled to keep up with the conversation. I stayed quiet, soaking in every word.

Her rejecting me served as an impetus for me to educate myself. It was even better than going to school in some ways. I was in the company of brilliant, creative, intellectual people, listening to them move effortlessly from English to Spanish and French, discussing layered, heady subjects. At times, I turned my head aside and repeated a sentence I'd just heard, helping it sink in as part of my learning. I don't know if anyone noticed.

Cuernavaca

Cuernavaca (originally *Cuanuhnahuac* in the Aztec language Nahuati) is lush and has an ideal climate year-round. To get there, visitors must climb out of the mountain-rimmed bowl that contains Mexico City and drive south.

The house in Cuernavaca was on Cerrado de Rufino Tamayo. Maka did not have riches. She was not wealthy. Her home was her prized possession and the only thing she had of real, monetary value. It had a pool and a lovely garden with bougainvillea, hibiscus, and poinsettia growing everywhere.

The house was medium-sized with an easy layout and pleasant proportions. The cool, smooth talavera stone floors were a pleasure to walk on with bare feet. Each room featured design details of arches and coves and strong colors such as burnt orange, turquoise, red, and cobalt blue. There were skylights in the hallways and bathrooms that allowed the sun to bathe the interiors with light. Tasteful antique wooden furniture was spread throughout the four-bedroom house. Maka's parents had left the house to her. Count Czernichew and Rosa Maria Dorantes lived their twilight years in this house in Cuernavaca, entertaining people like Helen Hayes.

The seven of us spent many weekends together in Cuernavaca. Michel, Demian, and I, along with Michel's brother Enrique, his wife Tita, and their son Alejandro. First thing in the morning, Maka expected us to meet in her bedroom. She held court as she sat up in her bed with a breakfast tray in front of her. We took up positions around her on various lounge chairs and stools. She directed the conversation, throwing out questions on current events or literary figures, or quoting lines from well-known poems, expecting us to respond intelligently.

Michel and Enrique had gone through this their entire lives; they were both eloquent and well-read. Tita and I looked at each other and raised our eyebrows in recognition that neither of us knew what Maka was talking about. She intimidated Tita to the degree that she later decided to close herself off from the world, stay in her apartment for a year, and do nothing but read. Maka oversaw the reading list. Tita became a successful movie producer, perhaps inspired by the stories she read under Maka's gaze.

The venerable painter Rufino Tamayo and his wife, Olga, lived next door. They never visited our house—Maka was likely embarrassed by her two less-than-intellectual daughters-in-law—but she went to see them often. As the first female abstract expressionist in Mexico, Maka was a contemporary of Tamayo. By that time, she had exhibited at Bellas Artes and El Museo de Arte Contemporáneo.

She had also hosted a television program called *Encuentro,* where she interviewed renowned writers, filmmakers, and other cultural figures, and was by then highly respected in those circles.

The weekends in Cuernavaca, with the prevalent exposure to the intellectuals and talented bohemian friends that came to visit, impacted me greatly. I had never been around such cultured, highly educated people. They discussed books, art, music, and filmmaking. Their vocabulary was vast. By then, I was fluent in Spanish, but they used words I had never heard before.

Many years later, I would live in New York and enroll in a self-designed degree program at New School University. I was determined to fill the gaps in my education that became apparent through my interactions with Maka. I wanted to remedy the cultural inferiority complex she gave me. I took courses in French literature, Greek and Roman history, writing, and art. I began collecting Mexican art, enchanted by Tamayo's paintings and those of Gunther Gerzo, Pedro Coronel, Francisco Toledo, Siquieros, and others I had had the privilege to know, well, at least observe, during my time living in Mexico.

Thank you, Maka, for spurring me on to exercise my mind as well as my body. Our uncomfortable time together turned out to enrich my life. It wasn't easy being around her. I now appreciate the value of her influence.

Downward Facing Dog is an inversion. During this period of my life, the people I met, Carol, Baba, Michel, and Maka, turned my life upside down, causing me to expand my consciousness and my culture. I gazed inward not only to my third eye, but to my mind. My life took an esoteric turn through a spiritual awakening during these years. My curiosity for higher learning was activated—the third eye governs the brain, the intellect—and sparked my lifelong quest to study and read, to be knowledgeable and able to discuss subjects of intellectual interest.

My years-long hatha yoga practice rose to another level, a higher, existential form that sustained and supported my journey, outward and inward. I hold physical postures for extended periods of time. I access a divine, blissful stillness. I sit in that stillness without noticing my body, and the solace I feel in meditation soothes me. I know there is more. I have only begun to understand the reason I am here. I can't go back. My journey through life would forever be infused with a resounding, heightened awareness.

9. Purgatory

If you are going through hell, keep going.

—Winston Churchill

Forward Bend
Uttanasana

Uttana means intense. It is a posture used to relieve stress and soothe the nervous system. This is the same posture as in Chapter 3, only this time we are initiating the return, back through the same flow of postures to the original one. From Downward Facing Dog, you can jump or walk up to meet the hands, landing in Uttanasana, bowing, feeling the deep stretch along the entire backside of the body, head down, folding into yourself, a gesture of reverence to our star, the Sun.

Crown Chakra
Sahasrara ~ thousand petaled

The color used to represent the Crown Chakra is violet or white. It is most often looked upon as our connection to the divine. It is a portal to the higher self, a bridge to the cosmos, governing transformation and the understanding of our true nature. It helps you feel compassion for others. It represents devotion and unity. When expanded, it helps us to reach our highest potential and to trust in the universe. It is located at the crown of the head and, in many traditions, is depicted as a halo.

The Phone Call

In the summer of 1985, I took Demian to the Siddha Yoga Ashram in South Fallsburg, New York. My friend and her daughter joined us. I was taking yoga teacher training. All of us participated in the activities that life in the ashram offered: meditating, chanting, doing our seva, and eating satiating vegetarian food. The landscape was picturesque and idyllic, nestled in the Catskill Mountains, where the air carried the freshness of pine and hemlock, laced with the sweet, wintergreen scent of birch and the earthy perfume of moss and river water.

The sweet smell of Nag Champa incense hung over the lobby of the ashram. I was waiting near the pay phone for Demian's pediatrician to call. The phone rang loudly, a disturbing noise in the serene sanctuary. I answered, listened, and heard the most crushing, heart-wrenching words: "Your son has leukemia." My breath quickened, a heavy flood of sorrow surged from my chest and spread through the rest of my body. The doctor continued to say that Demian had to be hospitalized immediately. "His blood counts are at dangerous levels. What would you like to do?"

Wait. Wait. This cannot be happening to my beautiful four-year-old son. His birthday, July 3, had just passed. The day after, we gathered with friends, watching the fireworks burst into the night. I noticed that something was off. I looked at my son's face. His expression was serious and solemn. The pain in his eyes was visible. There were other reasons to be concerned.

For weeks, I awakened to find him drenched, with his eyes open, lying there in bed. Why was he having night sweats? Then I noticed his stool was white. His complexion and his lips were chalky. Something was very wrong.

I had no idea how wrong.

Demian was getting nosebleeds at home in Mexico City, prior to arriving at the ashram. Worried, I took him to Dr. Lasky, his pediatrician, who assured me he was fine. "Probably the pollution," he said. Earlier that day, I took him to a local pediatrician for a second opinion. The doctor suspected something more than poor air quality was causing his symptoms when he felt the swollen nodes in Demian's neck.

I slowly hung up the phone after the gravity of the diagnosis hit me. Leukemia. I needed to talk to Gurumayi, Muktananda's successor, the current head of the Siddha lineage. How could this be happening in a place such as this? Where was the sanctity, security, and safety of the ashram? How could this fate strike an innocent four-year-old in a place where the divine Shiva and his consort Shakti, together with blessings from other deities, were invoked from morning to night?

Wait, wasn't Mt. Fuji thought to be sacred, too? Twenty years ago, it swallowed my parents in a plane crash. The worst crash in aviation history. Photos of the wreckage were featured in *Life* magazine. There was a picture of the plane in a nose-dive with smoke and debris and bodies trailing, plummeting down toward the sacred mountain. What was going through my parents' minds when they realized what was happening?

There was another photo in the magazine, taken the night before the crash, of the passengers who perished the next day. Many of them dressed in traditional Japanese robes, smiling, unaware of what awaited them. I spotted my dad, front row center, beaming, and Mom standing shyly near the edge of the photo. Unlike Dad, she was expressionless. I hurt for her, thinking she was afraid and joyless in her final hours. The most painful photo was the one showing the bodies lined up, covered in dark blankets on the ground. Knowing two of them were my parents made me feel raw and shaken to my core. How strange to have your tragedy covering the insides of something people buy off the rack at the grocery store.

Losing my parents and receiving Demian's diagnosis was too much catastrophe for one lifetime. I thought I paid my karmic dues. Since the plane crash, I comforted myself whenever I was flying and hit turbulence by thinking it couldn't happen twice in one family. Demian's diagnosis was possibly even more painful to me than losing my parents. He was my only child, and the doctor informed me he would suffer terribly and might not survive.

Grace of the Guru and Power of the Mantra

If OM contains the sound and power of the universe (when you pronounce the "O" beginning at the lips and finish the "M" at the base of the throat) and if "Om Namah Shivaya" contains the energy of the millions of people who have ever chanted, written, or thought it, I was going to put it to the ultimate test. Could it bring my son back from near death?

After the diagnosis, I was granted the rare privilege of meeting with Gurumayi. It took place within the sanctuary of her private quarters. I entered her room and felt the divinity of her presence spill over me. I had felt the same soft yet tingling electrical charge around Baba Muktananda years before in other ashrams. Her grace and loving gaze when I told her what was happening felt as if she were holding me in a warm ocean of calm. I was nervous and devastated, but somehow felt a sense of peace and hope during our conversation.

She asked me what options I had. I told her we could go back to Mexico City or stay with my aunt and uncle in Denver and start treatment there. Michel and I were still together but at a distance in a few ways. My work ethic seemed difficult for him to understand, and I perceived his inability to maintain consistent work as a lack of motivation. Michel was in entertainment; he produced a film and was out of work for the next six months. The sporadic nature of his work put a strain on our relationship, with me feeling responsible for our finances.

I didn't have health insurance in the US; only in Mexico. Gurumayi told me to go to Denver and that my aunt and uncle would help me. "Demian will survive," she said. I held on to those words through the next three years of brutal chemotherapy.

We made it to Denver, and Demian started treatment at Denver Children's Hospital. The doctors in the pediatric oncology department gave him a forty percent chance of survival and assigned him a random protocol: a schedule of fourteen drugs that meant he would be getting chemo every other week for three years. It was administered with cranial radiation treatments and more procedures I don't have words to describe. He endured it stoically.

During the difficult initial induction period, when they tried to eradicate the cancer cells along with many other cells, Demian slipped into a coma. He was in intensive care, his body limp, his eyes halfway open with a blank stare. He had lost half of his body weight and every hair on his body. The doctor advised me to call his father and ask him to come at once.

"Demian may not survive."

Michel rushed to Denver from Mexico City, where he was working on a film.

When Michel arrived, I had been awake for three days straight, tending to Demian in the hospital. Michel, the brilliant, witty, and engaging conversationalist I knew, withdrew from me—no doubt out of concern for our son. I needed to talk, and he needed silence. I felt emotionally isolated from him. Michel never had a father figure. I saw him struggling with how to handle the situation. I wondered if he avoided conversations with me because he was exhausted from tending to Maka.

I was in the maximum state of anguish a person can tolerate without stepping over the edge into total madness. How could this be happening? Gurumayi had assured me Demian would be okay. I telephoned the ashram and told Gurumayi's assistant what was happening. Gurumayi responded by telling me to play a tape she gave me for Demian. The tape was a departing gift of a special recording of herself chanting the mantra, "Om Namah Shivaya." I had a small portable cassette player with headphones that I placed on Demian's ears. I was alone with him in the ICU.

I chanted along with the voice of Gurumayi and prayed for a miracle. I watched his face, his eyes. Time passed. I'm unsure how long I sat there. I began to observe the life force reenter his body. He started blinking and attempting to move his fingers. He looked so small and weak, his skin had a lackluster, yellowish hue, hanging limply off his bones. Intubated and on life support, he was surrounded by wires hooked up to all kinds of equipment. But there he was, fighting to come back to life!

The mantra brought him back. I witnessed it. It was then that I truly understood the grace of the guru and the power of the mantra. Perhaps my determination to save my son also helped.

In those days, doctors didn't make statements of patients being cancer-free or in remission, but in so many words, they confirmed he was. "The further out, the less chance of relapse," they told me. The treatments continued, but the worst was behind us.

The Tortuous Years of Treatment

Demian continued to fight for his life after his near-death experience. Oddly enough, he never cried, at least not in front of me. He just screamed, a horrible, painful wail, when they removed his precious spinal fluid and replaced it with a shot of spinal methotrexate directly into his spine. This happened every two months. It was horrific to hear and watch. The scene is branded into my memory. I wished I could take the treatment for him to spare him the excruciating pain.

He bravely endured the nausea-producing chemo and the daily cleaning of the Broviac catheter, where his blood was constantly drawn, counts monitored, and meds administered. For almost three years, I cleaned his Broviac every day, injecting saline solution to prevent it from clogging. I kept the site where it entered his skin sanitized with alcohol to avoid infections. Countless times, I bolted upright in bed, gasping in the middle of the night, gripped by the fear I had forgotten to flush the Broviac. If it clogged, it meant yet another surgery to insert a new one. I looked upon it not solely as a lifeline to the treatment he needed but as an umbilical cord that connected us 24/7.

For the first year and a half back in Colorado, Demian and I lived at my aunt and uncle's house on Grape Street in Denver. It was the same house where I lived for those two and a half years when I was in high school at St. Mary's Academy. I'm sure they felt they had no choice but to help, although the house didn't come for free. My aunt insisted I pay $300 per month for rent out of my Medicaid check. My inheritance was long gone. I had food stamps, after all, didn't I? I couldn't help thinking my parents would never have charged me rent. The last thing I needed was another burden, like not having enough money.

I applied for Medicaid because we did not have US health insurance. Demian's three-year treatment was estimated to cost close to half a million dollars, considering the number of hospital stays and complications that would inevitably arise. Michel and I could not come up with that kind of money.

My aunt lent me her late-model Mercedes-Benz to drive to the welfare services office. She told me to park it out of sight because if someone saw me, I wouldn't get approved for benefits. I lined up with the other desperate, destitute people in a shabby office in downtown Denver and took a number. When I was called, I told them I had no money, no possessions, and no other choice but to ask for government assistance.

After the brutal induction and his near-death experience in the intensive care unit, I watched the rest of summer pass by from the second-floor window of Demian's room at Denver Children's Hospital. Being there was stressful, but I was grateful that the days went by without a major incident.

I was vigilant and rarely left Demian's side as I worried that something could go wrong. This fear began after I observed a nurse nearly give him a medication meant for the child in the next room. We are not talking about aspirin—these drugs were potent cancer meds.

I kept everything sterile around him, sometimes surreptitiously wiping down everything around him with alcohol wipes I kept in my purse. I wanted to sterilize anything I thought he might touch. If anyone came around, I observed them closely for signs of a cold or cough. Demian's immune system was constantly compromised. As soon as his blood counts recovered, they blasted them again with another round of chemotherapy.

Every two weeks, Demian had his blood drawn to detect the presence of any cancer cells. We had to wait 24 hours for the results. I suffered during that time, wondering if he would relapse. To this day, I am afraid of bloodwork, even for myself.

Then Demian started having seizures. They came with no warning signs. His eyes rolled up into his head, and he stopped breathing and turned blue. Once they passed, I was too afraid to take my eyes off of him for fear he would have another one and I wouldn't be there in time to inject him or rush him to the hospital. Sometimes I stayed up all night watching him, lying next to him, listening to the rhythm of his breath, praying he wouldn't have another one.

I harnessed one hundred percent of my being to help Demian. My days centered on his healing. I researched alternative homeopathic treatments, diets, and supplements. With a specialist, I taught him neurolinguistic programming—a therapeutic technique that uses language and visualization to shift perception—so he could transport himself to another place when he was experiencing pain. Anything and everything, with a remote chance of helping him, I tried. I ran my ideas by his doctors and nurses to make sure they didn't interfere with his prescribed protocol. They looked upon my constant quest as somewhat strange and rather futile. It didn't deter me.

During Demian's cranial and spinal radiation treatments, I watched through the window from an adjoining room, focusing on reciting the mantra and sending healing, protective thoughts to him. I summoned my will and directed it toward him. I envisioned Baba Muktananda, Gurumayi, and any other saint who came to mind encircling him, protecting him.

I read that packs of miso, the base ingredient of Japanese soup, help draw out impurities when applied to the stomach. At one point, Demian developed a severe fungus that made him excrete this vile, black, foamy substance. I applied miso to his belly. The doctors thought I was a lunatic. I think it helped. Desperate for the healing smell of the ashram, I burned incense in the hospital until they told me to get rid of it.

I developed a yoga routine for constipation for him, as the chemo affected his ability to move the little food he was eating out of his body. Most of it came out as vomit from his constant nausea.

I am convinced that my efforts to incorporate alternative treatments made a positive difference. He had fewer hospitalizations than most of the other kids, and he never relapsed, but he missed out on important aspects of his childhood.

Demian rarely went to school that first year. He was too sick or his immune system was too compromised, so I taught him myself. I researched what children were supposed to be learning at age five and compiled the curriculum. He tried his best, but most of the time, he was foggy, finding it difficult to focus and retain information.

I did all I could to make a normal life for my son.

I made a Halloween costume for him, crying as I sewed, thinking it might be his last. It was a cozy, padded baby-blue bear suit, with a big stuffed headpiece that framed his face and covered his bald head, keeping his frail, thin body warm. Except for his yellowish, pale skin and the absence of eyebrows and lashes, he looked almost normal in it.

Being in public was challenging. We didn't leave the house much because Demian's blood counts were so low that he was at risk of catching anything. With no immune system, the doctors warned he was vulnerable to innocuous viruses like measles. "If that happens, he could die," they said.

When we did venture out, say, early in the morning to the supermarket (I figured the space was empty all night so there'd be less risk of contracting something), the stares from people due to his baldness and frailness were hard for both of us to endure. At four, he had the eyes of a wise old man. Sensitive and empathetic by nature, he absorbed every stare and every comment whispered behind his back.

We went to the hospital for Demian's infusions—the kind where the chemo had to drip slowly over time, rather than the ones we pushed through his Broviac catheter at home. We gathered with the other children undergoing treatment. The parents talked and exchanged stories about our shared difficulties. Some had their insurance cancelled unexpectedly because one parent was fired from their job. That happened often. Others were facing problems with their healthy children who were unintentionally being neglected. I'll never forget when one of them said, "When a child has cancer, the whole family gets cancer. Everyone suffers."

There we sat in a large sterile room, hovering over precious, severely ill children, hooked up to IVs full of toxic chemo. It was heartbreaking when a child's familiar face was absent the next week, only to find out they had died. Demian's survival rate was posited at forty percent, which didn't seem so bad compared to others with rare, untreatable cancers.

I found that when discussing the future of their cancer-stricken child, every parent maintained fierce faith that everything would be okay. It was far too painful, intolerable, to think otherwise. They held on to hope until the very end. My heart goes out to any parent who has experienced it. To see a vibrant, young child forcibly reduced to a weak, sickly, frightened being with no hair and an uncertain future is beyond words in its sadness.

My Rare Escapes

My only outlet during that time in Denver was teaching yoga at Cherry Creek Sporting Club three times per week. Since I was on welfare, I couldn't get paid, so I took Taekwondo classes in exchange for teaching. I punched and kicked with all of my might. There were only two women in class and roughly twenty men. I discovered, to my dismay, that the men enjoyed roughing us up. When we were sparring, they hit a little too hard. I was so heartbroken and beaten down that I almost expected it from them. I didn't give in, and I began to see it as a metaphor for what I was going through with Demian. I was unyielding, taking whatever life hurled at me, and I still had the strength to push back.

It was still 1985, and in nearby Boulder, Colorado, experimental healing techniques were being introduced. I enrolled in a sound healing class, hoping I could practice on Demian. The Cherry Creek Sporting Club offered free childcare, so I took him there while I attended class, though I was apprehensive about leaving him. I scanned the room, worried he might catch a cold from another child. If there were too many kids, or if someone sneezed or coughed, I skipped class, gathered him up, and we went back home. When everything worked out, I treasured that precious time—whether to teach yoga, practice Taekwondo, or take a healing class.

During the first year and a half of Demian's treatment, I did yoga at home every night, even when I didn't sleep for fear of him having a seizure. I did the hour and a half of 26 postures, Bikram's routine, that I had been practicing for over ten years. It saved me mentally, emotionally and kept me healthy enough to be a good caregiver. I never got sick once. There was nobody to step in if that happened.

Here I was in my early thirties, alone, caring for my critically ill son. My friends were enjoying their lives, involved in their children's school and after-school activities. They were watching their children grow and flourish while I was alone, focused on keeping my son alive. I didn't allow myself to get depressed. I didn't have that luxury. I had to stay strong and positive and show my son that everything was going to be alright. He was going to live.

Back to Los Angeles

How different this time in LA was for me. Last time it was the '70s. I was carefree—dating and disco dancing—with lots of money from the Boeing settlement.

Now, we were halfway through the ruthless three-year protocol. We transferred to the pediatric oncology department at the University of California, Los Angeles for the final half of his treatment because Michel found work in Los Angeles.

Up to this point, he hadn't helped me much beyond supportive phone calls. His freelance television work in Mexico City was sporadic, and frankly, I knew he couldn't face what was happening to his son.

We packed up and moved to LA, but the family reunion proved to be short-lived. Michel didn't like Los Angeles, especially commuting in traffic. Even though he had a job he enjoyed at an advertising agency in Laguna Niguel, he couldn't take it anymore. After a year, he moved back to Mexico City, leaving Demian and me to carry on once again.

The support of my friends and the joy of teaching yoga during this period carried me through the excruciating ordeal of seeing my son undergo cancer treatment. A friend whom I knew from Mexico City was now living in San Diego. She fled Mexico City with her husband and three boys after being held at gunpoint for hours in their home while thieves scavenged their home, taking everything they found, including names and phone numbers of potential future victims.

Now, they were safe in their new home. A year and a half into Demian's treatments, she offered to have him stay with them overnight. My friend had nursing skills—she could flush Demian's catheter—and offered me a night off. Demian could play with their three boys. They picked him up in Los Angeles and took him to San Diego.

No one had offered that type of help. The gesture moved me. I thank her from the bottom of my heart.

Giving back

When we eventually moved back to Mexico City a few years later, I volunteered in the pediatric oncology department at one of the public hospitals. I taught yoga to the parents of the children undergoing treatment and spent time with the children who had no visitors. Their parents had to work and take care of the rest of their children. Some of them were extremely poor, illiterate farmers and peasants from rural Mexico who didn't fully comprehend what was happening. They barely spoke Spanish, only their local dialects. I did my best to communicate to them that there was hope. I told them I experienced what they were going through and that my son had survived.

Working there, I realized how lucky we were to have private rooms at Denver Children's Hospital and the research hospital at UCLA, where Demian concluded his treatment. In Mexico, there could be twelve children in a room. With a compromised immune system, it was a dangerous situation. A cold could turn into pneumonia and become fatal.

LA: The Yoga Mecca

Bikram told me in those early years that I was not allowed to teach any style of yoga but Bikram. If I did, he would never speak to me again. So many years later, I didn't care; I wasn't in touch with him anymore. I was eager to experience other styles of yoga that people were talking about.

I saw Bikram in Vail, many years after we met. He was giving a workshop at the invitation of one of his students. He was cordial but distant when he saw me. By then, his ego had taken over, and he praised himself incessantly. His gaze had hardened, and he lost his boyish innocence and charm. I still looked upon him with a sense of gratitude. He gave me the greatest gift. Yoga saved my life and provided me with a career.

When I moved beyond Bikram yoga, or Hot Yoga as people call it today, I began to explore other disciplines. Maty Ezraty and Chuck Miller opened the biggest, brightest studio on Montana Avenue in LA called Yoga Works, where they taught Ashtanga yoga.

Vigorous and demanding, Ashtanga involves synchronizing movement with the breath and incorporating the use and control of bandhas, or energy locks of the body, in a fixed sequence of postures practiced in prescribed order that allows for connective flow. It requires jumping through the hands from Downward Facing Dog to a seated position to execute a posture, then lifting the body weight and shooting the legs back through the arms to Chaturanga or Grasshopper Pose. Not an easy feat. I liked Ashtanga and practiced it diligently until I finally jumped through my hands and landed softly on my butt.

I was so lucky to be teaching in the yoga mecca of the world at the time: Montana Avenue in Santa Monica, California, circa 1987. Only a few million people practiced yoga in those days in the United States. Today, there are over 60 million.

We were pioneers, introducing the ancient practice of yoga to the masses. Many of the teachers at the time became famous. We were teaching, taking each other's classes, and sharing ideas. It was incredibly thrilling to be a part of the yoga scene. It was in its nascent stage of becoming palpable for mass consumption. From LA, it would spill across America and the world, seep into the curriculum of local gyms and fitness centers, and become a regular ritual in the lives of so many people.

After almost a decade of solely teaching the Bikram yoga 26 posture sequence, I was liberated. I took what I was learning from other teachers, interpreted it, ran it through my body to experience the sensations myself, and taught in my unique way. I played music from Enya during class, came up with a new order of postures, and connected them creatively. I choreographed sequences and brought in new elements, influenced by my years of dance and gymnastics.

I developed a new language when leading a class. I read the room and sensed who was ready to step it up with more advanced postures and who came to relax and unwind, better served with grounding floor postures with longer meditative holds.

A yoga teacher develops better intuition the more they teach—if they are doing it with the pure intention of helping people. Over the last two decades, I have taken classes where the teacher can't take their eyes off themselves in the mirror. In the '80s, in the yoga mecca of LA, there were no mass teacher trainings. Finding an experienced, qualified teacher wasn't easy, and teaching yoga wasn't as common a career path as it is today.

During this time, I took night classes once a week at UCLA. They offered a new certification program to become a fitness trainer. As I was the first person Bikram trained to become a teacher, he hadn't yet developed a curriculum that included anatomy and biomechanics. I needed a deeper understanding of this to teach properly. I wanted to know the name of every muscle, the proximal and distal attachments, and function. This certification program included courses on the psychology of exercise, nutrition, adult exercise theory, and sports performance. I felt blissful, except that when the other students and teachers learned I was a yoga instructor, they quickly dismissed my ideas.

There was no respect for yoga as an athletic tool. If I described the benefits of a posture and how it related to sports performance, for example, my classmates and professors rolled their eyes. But that was okay. The idea intrigued me, and a concept was brewing in my head. As a former competitive gymnast and sports enthusiast, I related yoga to these endeavors.

Mark Spitz, the Olympic champion swimmer, asked me for private classes. His back was bothering him. He wondered how yoga could help. I worked with him for a time, and he saw results—less pain and increased mobility. I was formulating what later became The Yoga for Athletes Fitness System, designed to improve performance, reduce the risk of injury, and increase the rate of recovery. These days, yoga is an integral part of many professional sports training programs. I like to think my work contributed in a meaningful way.

Ana Forrest

When I first met Ana, she reminded me of a sage, tribal woman. Her brown hair was twisted into two long braids that hung to her waist. Her face was prematurely weathered and lined as though she lived outdoors all her life. Her gaze was penetrating and focused. Ana's body was perfectly proportioned and equally strong and flexible.

She opened Forrest Yoga Studio, teaching her own unique style of yoga a few blocks away from the other studios, Yoga Works and Studio West, on Montana Avenue. Baron Baptiste, a young, well-known yogi even then, and I taught classes there.

Ana's method of diving into emotional trauma through her well-designed and unique yoga routines was intense, rather painful, and powerful. People released emotional trauma in her classes, sometimes by screaming or crying. There wasn't any New Age music playing in the background. This was a serious class, unlike my teaching, which was considered intense in terms of difficulty, but light and fun.

I personally experienced the pain and joy of release in her class one day when she suddenly turned and focused her gaze on me. Settled into Pigeon Pose—a posture that opens the hip joint—I rested comfortably, my head turned to one side and supported by my hands. She walked over, hovered above me, and then, while I watched her, stepped her foot onto my right hip, pressing her weight upon me as she stared into my eyes. She held her foot steady and firm until she felt I had released whatever was trapped in there.

When she let up, I felt something inside of me release. I don't know what it was—maybe just relief that she had removed her foot—but when I moved around after class, my hip felt different. Better. Freer. Ana had the keen ability to sense energy blocks and trauma in a person's body, and she knew what needed to be done to release it. Her background as a horse trainer and her connection to animals gave a distinct edge and depth to her teaching.

I regarded Ana as my idol in terms of the way she did the postures. Her control and mastery of the many variations of headstands and handstands were unlike anyone else I had ever witnessed. She placed her hands with steady assurance on the floor, and slowly, with consummate control and without bending her knees, raised her legs to a split position until they hovered just above the level of her head and extended to opposite sides of the room. She spread her toes and remained there, unwavering and completely still for as long as she wanted.

You could feel the energy running out through those pointed, sprawled-out toes. She continued to talk normally from this position. When she was ready to come down, she descended slowly, with the same mesmerizing grace. She stood up and gazed around at her students' faces, knowing she had impressed them.

Nobody did a handstand like Ana Forrest. It was awesome to watch.

Rod Stryker

Rod Stryker led the dreamiest guided meditation sessions. I took his classes at Yoga Works. His voice and energy were soothing and magical. He took a room packed with fifty people into a blissful state with his breathing techniques, poetic words, and voice. Many women were vying for his attention while seeking enlightenment.

I allowed myself to be taken on an inner journey with Rod's clear enunciation and deep soothing voice. It was different from meditating in a Siddha Yoga ashram, with the influence and traditions of Hinduism and Kashmir Shaivism apparent. This was a guided meditation that changed daily. It was in English, using words and phrases that describe the inner landscape of the mind, body, and soul in a more modern, contemporary way. While he referenced the Vedas (an ancient Sanskrit text) or other sacred scriptures from India, it felt as though he was presenting them for today's world, reframing meditation for modern-day consumption. I sensed an eagerness and excitement in the room, a collective feeling of truly being onto something. Meditation for the masses was being born.

Rod's contribution to yoga has been immense. He has taught for decades. I recently saw him after almost 30 years. I took a weekend workshop with him. It was sublime, reminding me of seeing a retrospective of an accomplished painter. In many cases, a painter, in their later years, begins to paint more simply, having reached the pure essence of expression, no longer needing embellishment.

That is how I felt when I took Rod's class this time. He took me deep into the postures with a few precise, well-chosen words. There was nothing superfluous, only the pure spirit of the pose. It was profound and moving. I felt weightless and free after the class, not exhausted from doing so many postures clustered together. It was purifying and wonderful.

Paul Grilley

Paul Grilley, who today is famous for the ubiquitous Yin Yoga, asked me if I wanted to join a small group of teachers that gathered three times per week for two-hour sessions. Not knowing this then, we were his testing lab where he was developing the meditative, deep, connective-tissue-activating school of yoga that he eventually named Yin. He wasn't sure what would come of it, but he knew he was onto something. How could I say no to the opportunity?

Dr. Drew Francis, a well-regarded Doctor of Oriental Medicine (OMD) who specializes in acupuncture, Suzee, who later became Paul's wife, a handful of other advanced yoga practitioners, and I gathered in a small back room at Studio West and did yoga together under Paul's observant eye. Guinea pigs. He wanted to know: What happens when you hold a shoulder stand for 20 minutes? What is the most effective hip opener and the ideal time to hold it (shattering previous conceptions of the ideal 30-second to one-minute hold)? Is internal rotation of the hip as essential as external rotation for maximum functionality? Can everyone eventually do a backbend if they practice long enough, or does bone structure—specifically the spinous process—impose limitations on that outcome?

During this developmental phase, Paul spent time with cadavers, took courses on anatomy, and focused on comparing basic bone structure in different people's bodies. Contrary to what many yoga teachers were telling their students ("if you do this posture enough times, you will eventually get there"), Paul found that everyone's unique bone structure could be a limiting factor in doing postures. The findings meant not all people could do all postures, even if they kept at it for years. Bone against bone, impossible. This was an important discovery and a relief for some who found they could not progress in certain postures.

Can a yoga teacher make a decent living?

I had to make money to support myself and Demian. Medicaid covered his final treatments. This pressure forced me to think of alternative ways to expand my teaching, and I cultivated an expansive base of private students. At the end of my public classes, when everyone was dreamily relaxing in savasana, I discreetly announced I also offered privates for anyone interested.

My clients were wealthy people who afforded the (then) hefty charge of $75 per hour plus driving time. I went to their palatial homes in Beverly Hills, Pacific Palisades, Malibu, and Hollywood to teach them yoga and give them Passive Yoga Therapy. William Shatner, Captain Kirk from Star Trek, was a regular. My clients loved Passive Yoga Therapy. Paul Grilley found a bunch of papers stapled together with diagrams and instructions on this method. He eagerly showed it to me and Drew as though he had found a map to a hidden treasure. Drew, Paul, and I practiced on one another. It was a variation of Thai massage, using one's own body weight to stretch and massage the client. We had never seen or heard of anything like it. We used our elbows to access deep areas that held tension and applied pressure by standing on the client. "What a relief," everyone said. "I don't have to do anything but lie on the floor and get flexible! When can you come back for another session?"

With my colleagues and students, I was in absolute yoga nirvana. Obsessed with creating new posture variations and choreographing fresh sequences, I poured myself into the work. My teaching took place at Studio West and Ana Forrest Yoga, where most days I led three public classes along with three or four private ones.

My new life was electrifying, but at times I felt my energy wane. I constantly had Demian on my mind. I rushed home between classes, checked in to make sure everything was okay, doled out instructions to the sweet babysitter I hired, and rushed back off to teach. I was astonished at how much I could do in one day. Here I was, a single mom of a child in remission from leukemia, working full time, attempting to create a career.

Kathy Smith, the well-known fitness instructor with a perfect body and her own fitness empire of TV shows, videos, and equipment, wanted private classes. The word was spreading fast, and my classes were full.

After months of working together, Kathy asked me to develop a style of yoga to teach in a gym setting. Reebok was opening a new, stunning gym in West LA. She was a part of it and wanted me to create something to get the gym rats off the stair climbers and into a yoga class.

I had gained a reputation for giving a challenging class, but I needed to elevate it even further to generate more interest. I added pushups to the chaturangas, longer holds on balancing postures, and clever, intricate connections between postures—faster, harder, heat, and sweat. I called it Power Yoga. It was a huge success. Reebok's Mezzeplex Gym was an experimental lab filled with the latest equipment. Everything was shiny and new, painted black and white with mirrors strategically placed so you could see yourself and everyone else. The circular yoga room was center stage, lit up with theater-like halogen lighting, lined with jagged mirrors at odd angles. Not exactly a conventional teaching space. This type of environment was brand new, and the buzz around the class swelled. The room was packed. Traditional yoga was being taken into another dimension.

These scenes would replicate and spread across the US and the world. In the years following this creative burst of yoga in the Western world, millions of people who had never imagined themselves doing yoga became devoted practitioners. I felt lucky then, and even more in retrospect, to have been a part of it.

At the peak of my yoga career in LA, Demian started telling me he longed for his father and he needed to be with him. After all he had endured, I wanted to give him anything he asked for. I was uncertain of his future; there was a looming possibility of a relapse. If he wanted to be with his father, I would drop everything and move back to Mexico. It wasn't what I wanted, but his needs were my number one priority.

When I left Mezzeplex, they brought in Brian Kest, whom I have only met twice, to take over my beloved Power Yoga classes. He expanded the concept and became a huge success. On one hand, I was happy my concept continued to take hold and become more and more popular. On the other hand, I had pangs of remorse over the success, and it hurt not to be given credit or even a mention.

Since then, my attitude toward proprietorship has changed.

Once you put something out into a yoga class, you cannot control it. The true sentiment should be one of joy when many people find something valuable enough to copy and continue. It is the nature of everything, really. It enters the realm of another person's consciousness, and once it has meshed with their particular view, they bring their own lens and character to it.

Uttanasana Forward Bend is an intense stretch for the entire backside of the body. The Crown chakra controls the connection to your higher self. It gives you compassion. This period of my life was intense. My only child received a cancer diagnosis. Any parent who has lived through such an ordeal will agree that the magnitude of such an experience will expand your ability to feel compassion far beyond anything you imagined. To witness an innocent child suffering still brings tears to my eyes.

I had the opportunity to deepen my hatha yoga practice, creating a portal to the higher self with learning and experiencing many teachers like myself. Through fierce persistence, a door opened. I was going through hell, but kept moving forward. It was a time of growth and expansion: physically, emotionally, and spiritually.

Uttanasana is a corporeal representation of this stage of my life: dropping down to the furthest point the body will go without breaking to turn within as deeply as possible. Being struck down with my son's cancer diagnosis forced me to do that in search of the strength to survive. In this posture, we are graciously bowing down to accept the challenges that life presents, showing reverence to the unfathomable higher forces at work and trusting it's all part of the journey leading to self-realization.

10. Reinvention

A bend in the road is not the end of the road . . . unless you fail to make the turn.

—Helen Keller

Half Standing Forward Bend
Ardha Uttanasana

Ardha means half. Uttana means intense. Asana means pose. Inhale as you raise your head to gaze forward, but only to the point where your palms lift off the ground and your fingertips remain anchored. Tilt the sacrum to deepen the stretch, lengthening the muscles throughout the backside of the legs. Create a deep curve in the spine, completely changing its shape from the previous posture. Press your shoulders firmly away from your ears, allowing space for the upper chest and throat to open.

Higher Heart Chakra
Hridaya ~ spiritual heart

A beautiful aquamarine color, a combination of the green heart chakra and blue throat chakra. This chakra, a bridge between the heart and throat, is associated with profound healing and deeper compassion and holds tremendous transformative power. It regulates the act of halting speech when a particular emotion arises, allowing discernment so that authentic expression can be achieved. It is associated with true healing by letting go of resentment and anger and moving forward with a lighter heart. It is located over the thymus gland above the heart.

Back to Cuernavaca

LA to Cuernavaca, quite a change. I was concerned about the air pollution in Mexico City. I thought Cuernavaca was a good option, approximately one hour from Mexico City. Demian and Michel could be together on the weekends.

I rented a house sight unseen, one of those coincidences that occur and instinctively assure you that you are on the right track. I heard about a Mexican couple looking for a tenant for their house in Cuernavaca. They were expanding their business in the States, designing bold sterling silver belt buckles.

Michel and I determined that Demian could not drive down with me. It was too risky; he was fragile. One of my yoga students heard I was moving to Mexico. She wanted to spend some time in Mexico and agreed to drive with me. She didn't know what she was getting into. Neither did I.

We started off early one morning, drove to Texas, and found an adequate motel near the border. The next morning at dawn, we crossed into Mexico through customs. It was a large, dark, ominous structure near Ciudad Juárez, and the experience was scary. Here we were, two women traveling alone, entering rural northern Mexico with no idea of what to expect. I was aware of a lot of men lingering around, smoking and staring at us.

Once we crossed the border, the main thoroughfare degenerated into a dilapidated highway laced with never-ending potholes. It was two-way traffic with no shoulder space. Trucks, buses and motorcycles passed precariously with little regard for oncoming traffic.

We stopped for gas somewhere in the middle of nowhere. The people didn't even speak Spanish, just their local dialect. I managed to fill up without getting harassed by the men staring curiously at us, and off we went again. By then, I was driving fast because I was unsure if there were safe motel accommodations. I knew we couldn't spend the night in one of the remote, forsaken towns we were passing. I smelled the danger. Off in the distance, we saw dusty brown mountains, great mesas, and miles and miles of desert. I kept driving using a AAA foldout paper map as a guide until we reached Cuernavaca 24 hours later. My yoga student, cowering in the passenger seat, was completely freaked out by then.

The new house in Cuernavaca was not too far from the charming colonial house on Cerrado de Ruffino Tamayo, where years before, Michel, Demian, and I had spent our weekends with Maka. The grand, stately house we rented had seen better days. Surrounded by a garden and a substantial cement pool painted pale blue, it had white stucco walls with an orange tile roof. The first floor was locked up. It housed extra furniture and the cucarachas that scurried around everywhere at night. I loved the smooth terracotta stone tile, the same as the flooring in Maka's house. There were three sizable bedrooms with high ceilings and windows trimmed with lace curtains. The house was brimming with Mexican colonial furniture and colorful Mexican crafts of all kinds, brightly painted clay pots, and paintings.

The wild, lush garden was home to splendidly gnarly trees that held creeping vines of violet and yellow flowers. The overall impression was that of a garden that was given free rein to meander and grow wherever it pleased. It reminded me of something in a Gabriel Garcia Marquez novel where you could expect odd magic to occur.

One day, a few weeks after we arrived, I was wandering the garden and came upon a large insect I will never forget. It stopped me in my tracks. In Spanish, it is called *cara de niño* or "face of a child." It is the scariest creature I have ever seen with its strikingly misfit body, compiled of various body parts that don't seem to match—an odd mix of animal, insect, and human. I couldn't comfortably enjoy the garden after that face-to-face encounter, and I never let Demian walk around alone in it! That was all he needed in his fragile state of recovery, a bite from such a startlingly strange insect!

A black and white Great Dane named Lucy was included with the house rental. She had a yellow rubber duck she carried everywhere, pretending it was her nursing pup. She was the perfect reflection of the personality of the house: somewhat eccentric, scattered, and slightly forgotten.

We were able to locate Hermalinda, our beloved housekeeper and nanny, who lived with us before Demian's diagnosis. She loved Demian and broke down crying when she saw him. His hair had grown a bit after falling out and regrowing four or five times during the three years of his treatment. He was thin, his complexion ashen, and his gaze tentative. He wasn't the energetic, beaming child that she had said goodbye to five years before.

She cooked his favorite foods: *sopa de fideo*, *croquetas de jamón y queso*, and her delicious *frijoles negros* with *epazote*. Hermalinda couldn't stop hugging Demian, and he was overjoyed to have her back in our family.

There, I started from scratch again. I learned a lot teaching yoga in LA and had built up a large following of avid students. I had created a successful career for myself. I didn't know anyone in Cuernavaca, but I would have to find a way. I remembered my Dad's words, "You can do anything if you put your mind to it." Well, that had certainly been tested, working full-time, raising a child with cancer. Frankly, after that, nothing seemed that daunting.

I did have one big issue that needed to be resolved. I had no working papers. Michel and I had divorced the year before. Living apart, the stress of having a child struggling to survive, and my disappointment in what I perceived as his lack of support had all taken their toll on our relationship. But now I needed to be married to a Mexican or else I wouldn't be able to work. I had gone through the long, tedious process of applying for working papers years before, but now I didn't have time to do that. It wasn't a guarantee I could even get them again. I needed money.

Edmundo

Along came the debonair *galán* Edmundo Calanchini. He was the epitome of Ralph Lauren style with a touch of Latino. Everyone knew him for his men's clothing store in Mexico City, the eponymous Calanchinis. Buttery suede blazers in caramel, tan, and rust, white crisp linen shirts, gabardine slacks, riding pants, and tall leather boots comprised "the look."

For more formal wear, a man who shopped at Calanchinis could have a bespoke suit made from one of the finest fabrics that Edmundo imported from Italy. He sold smooth leather briefcases, wallets, and gloves and designed discreet flat gold chains meant to be worn with a barely buttoned shirt.

I met him at a friend's 40th birthday party held in Valle de Bravo, a weekend getaway spot for the affluent upper class of Mexico City. Valle (pronounced vie-yay), as they call it, is surrounded by mountains and fragrant pine trees that wrap around the pristine Lake Avandaro—a famous year-round destination, known for millions of monarch butterflies migrating there from Canada and the US in the winter. All of my old friends, expats and Mexicans alike, were among some 60 people at the birthday party at Juantepec Ranch. The ranch belonged to friends who were part of a close circle of expats.

It was a weekend filled with lively events, horseback riding, water skiing, and long, tequila-infused luncheons that lasted well into the night. The afternoon degustations started out slowly, sipping tequila to open the appetite, followed by a sprawling course of guacamole, *ceviche de pescado*, and *jamón serrano*. The main course was *tacos de pollo* (chicken), *champiñones* (mushrooms), and *rajas* (chiles) *con queso* (cheese) wrapped in warm, fresh handmade tortillas. It was difficult to choose a salsa for the final touch. They were delicious—*salsa verde, salsa mexicana, o salsa con chipotle y mayonesa.*

Between courses, all of us paused for a cigarette (most people smoked in those days). We called it an "intercourse cigarette." A few hours later, the main course arrived—dishes ranging from *chiles rellenos* to *falda de res* (skirt steak) to a rich mole. Another cigarette break, a few more *cervezas* or some tequila—or both—and finally dessert, usually creamy caramel flan or *pastel de tres leches* (three milks cake).

After what seemed like three days of one big continuous party, I came up for air. That's when I first connected with Edmundo. We didn't engage in deep conversation. It was a physical attraction. There were few words between us. Looking at him was like watching the attractive male yogis, sensing a radiance inside of myself from the outward emanation of theirs. No words, only movement. Edmundo and I were instantly flirtatious and playful.

Later that evening, one of my girlfriends asked me why I didn't have any makeup on. "Edmundo licked it off!" I said and fell forward laughing. Edmundo and I tumbled into a partnership for the next five years, lopsided, albeit, as I worked twelve-hour days teaching yoga, and doing ten haircuts a day at my new day spa. He found more pleasurable ways to spend his time, mainly in soothing me. After a long day at work, I would rest my head on his lap. He massaged my scalp and hair until I fell asleep. He helped with the cooking and keeping the house neat and decorated.

We got married. Even though we were wildly attracted to one another, I would not have married him if I didn't need my working papers. I doubt he would have married me had he not wanted a green card. I didn't want to live alone in Mexico. It seemed like an opportunity presented itself, so I went with it.

Cuernavaca was sparsely populated back then. I wouldn't be able to make a living teaching yoga and cutting hair. Besides, Edmundo lived in Mexico City. Off we went. I felt trepidation about living there as I was afraid the smog would affect Demian. But again, sometimes survival makes choices for you that override personal needs and wants.

Argie Hair Spa

I took my new yoga routines back to Mexico City. This time, I taught at my wonderful *locale* I called Argie Hair Spa. Edmundo and I opened it in the lovely, wooded, and upscale neighborhood of Lomas Altas on a street called Cumbres de Acultzingo. The area was full of large, expensive homes that surrounded the block with a few mid-rise apartment buildings like ours.

Located at street level, the hair spa had floor-to-ceiling windows. It looked out upon an estate across the street that had enormous carved wooden doors and high metal fences obscured by perfectly trimmed greenery. It served as protection for the former president Lopez Portillo's family.

Edmundo had vision. Together, we designed the space with large floating mirrors lit from behind, walls painted a soft peachy orange, and cream leather chairs. I put my meager savings into the project. Edmundo told me he was paying half of it. I later found out he had borrowed his half and then paid off the loan with money that came in from my haircuts.

While I continued my rigorous work schedule, Edmundo counted the money coming in and rode horses most of the day, English style, with his friend, Javier Calleja. He often wore a white button-down shirt and a pair of tight-fitting riding pants selected from a stack of perhaps fifteen varying colors kept in his closet. He pulled on one of his tall leather boots and met Javier for a day of riding, honing their skills in preparation for show jumping. It is an exquisitely graceful sport that requires the horse and rider to be in perfect harmony as the horse jumps and remains momentarily suspended in the air before gliding over the obstacle and landing with precision and coordination. Preparing and maintaining perfect cadence requires a swift recovery. Javier had competed, representing Mexico in the Summer Olympics, and Edmundo aspired to ride like him.

First thing in the morning, six days per week, I opened the doors of the salon/yoga studio to a group of women who came to do yoga, chat, and meet their friends. The Mexican women were talkative. They couldn't help themselves from chit-chatting even while holding a yoga posture. The women who came to class were the wives of ambassadors and international executives and socialites. Because of them, the studio became a place to see and be seen. People lingered after class, lounging on the sofa, gossiping and complaining about their hired help, or staying for a manicure or blow-dry. Their chauffeurs waited for them outside.

Our apartment was on the fifth floor of the same building as Argie Hair Spa. When Edmundo wasn't riding, he was rearranging the furniture, painting a wall a different color, or tending to the numerous plants and trees he had bought, creating gorgeous, Ralph Lauren-like spaces.

I worked as hard as I had in Los Angeles, now cutting hair and running a business. I was too busy. One day, I paused and realized I hadn't left the building in three months. The yoga classes were packed, and I had a steady stream of people lined up for haircuts. My employees were booked, doing hair color, blow-dries, manicures, and pedicures.

It wasn't easy to run a business in Mexico, especially as a foreigner. For the first year, I trained a young woman named Alicia to cut hair. I spent my precious time with her, sharing as much knowledge as I could, thinking I was helping her build a career. Suddenly, she disappeared. She didn't call in sick. I heard nothing from her.

After a week, I grew concerned, but instead of hearing from her, I received an official letter informing me I was being sued for mistreating my employee. All I did was teach her how to cut hair. The claim was beyond infuriating. There was no way I was going to pay for something I didn't do. For the next six months, representing myself (I refused to pay a lawyer), I went to court and presented my case, appearing several times for interviews and meetings. Everyone told me the situation was futile, that this happened frequently. Foreigners were often targets for these kinds of lawsuits meant to extract money, and they never won. Well, I won. However, a week later, three strange men appeared one afternoon just as I was about to close the salon.

I was alone, tidying up and preparing to teach the evening yoga class. They asked if I was Argie Ligeros and told me if I didn't pay Alicia $30,000 US dollars, I would be the victim of some type of crime. I better pay, or I would be very sorry.

The threat scared me to death. What if they kidnapped Demian? I discussed it with Edmundo, and we decided there was no other choice but to pay. It was incredibly frustrating. People told me it's the price of doing business in Mexico. On one hand, I was successful, most likely beyond what I could achieve in the States, but it came with major difficulties.

I carried on and trained two other women to become yoga teachers during that period. Together, we opened a yoga studio nearby in Lomas de Herradura. We brought teachers such as Paul Grilley and Rodney Yee from the United States to do week-long intensives. We were creating a yoga community that embraced everything we offered.

Teaching this demographic required patience. I was used to pushing people's self-imposed limits. These women had limitations. Many had never exercised. It taught me to teach at a beginner level and understand that progress came slowly. Support and encouragement were vital. I often heard the phrase, "*Ay me duele!*" (Oh, that hurts). I had to respect that they were not used to even the slightest bit of discomfort. Most Mexican women had never participated in a gym class, let alone track and field or outdoor sports. They had never pushed themselves to the point of sweaty exhaustion. It illustrated to me the importance of physical education in childhood. There were exceptions, of course. It was gratifying to see them embrace their newly discovered physical potential.

Word spread about my yoga classes. I was invited to do guest television appearances, interviews, and magazine articles, demonstrating and discussing the new fitness phenomenon. I was bringing the knowledge and skills I gleaned and developed in Los Angeles to a wide audience in Mexico.

Even with my grueling schedule, I managed to maintain my personal yoga practice. I woke at 4:30 a.m., disguised myself to look like a boy, and rode my bike through Chapultepec Park. It was dark and dangerous, but I needed fresh air and movement. I was used to skiing, hiking, and biking outdoors.

Life was overwhelming. There was constant activity every minute of the day. Still, I was feeling productive and generating a healthy income, enough to make a down payment toward the purchase of my aunt and uncle's house in Frisco that they no longer wanted.

But resentment started to build. I was working much harder than Edmundo, a situation he seemed to enjoy. I held it in and blew up one evening when he announced he was going to buy a second horse. The money to pay for it came from my teaching and cutting hair. It wasn't fair. He didn't see it that way. I realized he was taking advantage of me.

Edmundo had other issues. He was moody. He went for days without saying a word to me, Hermalinda, or Demian.

I didn't know what to do. Demian was doing well. He was happy seeing his father on the weekends and attended a nearby private school called Westhill Institute. He walked there with Hermalinda and the children of a friend who lived in our building. The routine worked well until the principal at the school called to say, "You are crazy to let your kids walk to school. They could be kidnapped!"

Not only was I married to a guy who lived a life of leisure while I worked, it became apparent that Edmundo was still in love with his former girlfriend. He asked me to alter my appearance. His ex had silicone breasts. He requested I get implants, and I agreed even though I didn't want them. I wanted to please him, and many women were getting them. A friend of mine raved about her new breasts and gave me the name of her surgeon, and I jumped onto the table. I emerged unhappy with the decision, wondering how these foreign objects in my body would impact my yoga practice.

In Chapter 3, I find myself in this posture for the first time. I am attempting to look forward, curving the spine in a new direction, hyperextension, creating intense stretching in the backsides of the legs, through the front side of the torso. In the Sun Salutation, the postures become easier through repetition. This time around, the stretch is still extreme, but I have gained wisdom and strength. I create an even deeper curve in the spine. The muscles in the back of my legs are strong and stable, even when stretched to the maximum point. I gaze forward with my fingertips on the ground, a metaphor for the connection to the roots I have established that allow me to expand and look forward with confidence. Ardha Uttanasana is an intense forward bend and a backbend. During this period of my life, I can handle the changes: a move, a new business, and my demanding schedule that pulls me in many directions.

The Higher Heart Chakra must have been working overtime to regulate what I was feeling and what I was saying. For three years, every time Edmundo donned his riding pants, I refrained from saying anything. Every time a client sat in the chair for a haircut, I not only had to give the best haircut possible, I listened to their problems. Any hairstylist will tell you they are also a therapist. Many times I wanted to say, "Excuse me, I want to concentrate on cutting your hair rather than listening to you complain about your husband!" I had to refrain and keep smiling. It was exhausting, ten haircuts per day and two classes of yoga with ten or more students in each one.

If the thymus chakra regulates the endocrine system, I believe this is when I developed hypothyroidism that would show up in my late '60s. Working this much drained me. Somehow, I gained admiration and respect in the affluent community of wealthy Mexican women, ambassadors, and international expats whom my business served. I created a sought-after gathering space to see and be seen, learn the latest yoga routines, and get your hair and nails done, but it came at a cost to my health.

11. Prowess

Your work is to discover your work and then with all your heart give your-self to it.

—Buddha

Volcano Pose
Urdhva Hastasana

Continue rising to an upright position using the inhalation and momentum from the previous posture. Firmly contract the muscles in the back and the legs to maintain a flat back through the movement. The arms extend out to the sides, reaching as though gathering everything around and offering it up to something beyond. Pause at the apex, gazing upward at the palms directly overhead that have come together in a gesture of prayer.

Causal Chakra
Bindu ~ point

A silver glowing personal moon, it facilitates the flow of energy and light from the angelic realms. It is associated with enhanced psychic clarity and telepathic communication, thus enabling individuals to intuitively read the energy around them. It is located at the back of the head above the crown.

The Athletes of Vail, Colorado

In 1995, after three years of grueling yet gratifying work at Argie Hair Spa, I moved from Mexico City to Frisco, Colorado. There was a one-hundred percent devaluation of the peso at the end of 1994. That meant the imported products I sold at Argie Hair Spa doubled in cost. The mortgage on the new house I had just purchased from my uncle (yes, the pre-fab house in Frisco where I spent my weekends while in high school) also doubled. I was making pesos. My expat clients who relocated to open major companies in Mexico began getting transferred out, as doing business there changed with the devaluation of the peso. We had no savings to rely on and couldn't pay the mortgage on the Frisco house and the rent in Mexico City.

I felt like leaving Edmundo behind, but he convinced me it would be better if he came along. He would make improvements to the house and help out. He reminded me he still wanted his green card.

A year after I got the breast implants, I had them removed. They had obstructed my postures in yoga, and I couldn't stand them. During yoga, being in touch with my body, I felt them, but they didn't belong to me. In yoga, you're constantly scouring your body with your mind's eye. Lying on my stomach with two lumps on my chest that weren't there before, my body didn't feel right. Once they were removed, I felt lighter, more myself, happy with my modest breasts.

I had some friends and acquaintances living in Vail and conducted a weekend yoga intensive a few years earlier with fifty or more students. It was well-received, so I thought I could probably teach yoga and do haircuts on the side.

Poor Demian, he was doing well, but we had no other choice but to leave. We packed up, tearfully said goodbye to Hermalinda, whom we never saw again, and moved to Frisco, Colorado. It was January, and the winter of 1995 turned out to be a record year for snow.

Frisco was only a twenty-minute drive from Vail, unless the roads were snowy and icy. I faced dangerous driving conditions nearly every day that winter. The highway looked like a bobsled run with the snow piled up so high. I made that drive over Vail Pass twice a day, knowing I had students waiting for me in Vail each morning and Demian to care for when he returned home from school in Frisco.

I found teaching opportunities in two athletic clubs in Vail. The first class I taught, I looked out over a room of about twenty curious people who had shown up to see what yoga was all about. Most of them were ski instructors with outsized, overdeveloped quadriceps, chiseled flat abs, and broad, muscular shoulders, both men and women alike. When standing upright, their bodies leaned anteriorly due to tight hip flexors. They looked like they were in position, ready to ski down the mountain! This was the fittest group of students I had ever seen, yet it was obvious they could benefit from some yoga.

When I realized the stories behind the bodies in the room, I was intrigued. One such woman, Ellen Miller, became the only American woman to climb Mount Everest from both sides. She is one of five women in the world to achieve this. Her body was meant for forward motion with narrow hips, perfect proportions, and what looked like just about zero body fat. She moved surely and readily into the postures. It must have been liberating for her to stretch out those tight calf muscles and hip flexors.

I felt intimidated yet excited about the challenge of teaching such elite-level athletes. Remember, this was new to people. They had never done yoga before. I thought to myself that if I didn't get their attention with a bit of my athletic prowess, they wouldn't respect me. I sensed it and confirmed it after integrating into the local society. Most people living in Vail cared less about how much money you have. They cared about how well you ski or snowboard or perform in other outdoor activities. I had to get their attention. During those first classes, I gave brief demonstrations of some of the advanced postures and sequences, such as Crow jumping back into Chaturanga and Handstand to Scorpion. That piqued their interest and gave me a certain respect.

It took about six months to gain a following of students in Vail. I worked my way into another intense rhythm of teaching, similar to the one I had left behind in Los Angeles. Working with such fit, physically capable people invigorated my teaching. I took my instruction in a direction that seeded my studies at UCLA, where I began formulating yoga routines with sports and athletic training in mind. Now in Vail, I had the athletes to work with to further develop this new concept of implementing yoga postures to enhance sports performance.

Prisca

The Vail part of my story isn't complete without talking about Prisca. I met her early on when I was hired to work privately with two brothers, young aspiring ski racers, and their coach. Prisca was employed by the boys' father, had heard about my class, and decided to join us. After class, she invited me to go skiing with her the next day. I never saw anyone ski like her. She was fearless and graceful on the slopes, moving with a fluid strength that made even the most challenging runs look effortless. She had the energy of an athlete, the precision of a coach, and the heart of a true adventurer.

That day, we made a deal. She said, "You teach me to do yoga like you, and I'll teach you to ski like me." It was the beginning of a partnership that would shape both of our lives. Prisca had a spark—she was bold, funny, and endlessly creative. Her passion for movement and her curiosity about yoga matched my own, and together, we fed off each other's energy.

Over the years, we produced seven instructional yoga videos, conducted workshops, produced television programs, worked fitness fairs, and more. Prisca brought her natural charisma and confidence into everything we did—whether on camera, on skis, or on the mat. She had the gift of making people believe they could do more than they ever thought possible.

It has been a fantastic journey, collaborating, laughing all along the way, and having the best time. Beyond all the projects, what I cherish most is the friendship. Prisca remains a close friend and yoga partner— one of those rare people who come into your life and never leave.

Balance in Motion

What a joy to teach athletes. They knew their right from left without having to pause. They translated instructions quickly from their brain to their bodies and came equipped with the discipline to be consistent. I received positive reinforcement from these students. They were feeling better, performing better. A full, long day of teaching skiing would be considered brutal for the average person. Imagine doing it five or six days a week for the entire winter. Not only did they have fewer aches and pains, their skiing improved. They became hooked on yoga. My classes grew to an average of forty people per class. There was nobody else teaching in Vail. It was the mid-nineties, and yoga was still a novelty.

The most rewarding feedback I heard often in some variation or another was when a student would come to me and say, "Yoga saved me from what could have been a disastrous fall yesterday. Had I not been able to recover from being thrown off balance skiing over a protruding rock, I definitely would have fallen." Yoga had likely saved them from a serious injury.

Balance and proprioception were notably improving for everyone with the many balancing postures I incorporated into the sequences. I took a single balancing pose and connected it to another one without pausing to regroup by putting both legs on the ground. Connect one, two, and even three poses together in a flow. Why not? I started thinking about the demands placed on the body while participating in a sport. You aren't standing still! This translated into achieving greater "balance in motion." You must have balance when you are moving through space, whether on skis, a snowboard, or a bicycle. Balance can be learned, dispelling the notion of "Oh, I just don't have good balance."

And the benefit of being flexible—say, while cross-country skiing—translated directly into longer strides and therefore more power to increase speed. Greater hip flexibility in downhill skiing meant the ability to lean much more deeply into a turn. Think of those skiers navigating gates in a downhill race, their hips nearly touching the snow as they carve each turn.

Inspired by the experience of working with elite athletes, I wrote a book with Prisca, *The Yoga for Athletes Fitness System*. The system was designed to "improve your performance, lessen the risk of injury, and increase your recovery rate." I applied this when I worked with the US Ski & Snowboard Team and the US Bobsled Team. The same principles also worked in the many golf clinics and other sports-related workshops I taught.

Meanwhile, Edmundo got his green card, we divorced, and he went back to Mexico City. I still see him when I travel to Mexico. The attraction has worn off, but he remains pleasant to my eyes—the contrast of his tan against his white, linen shirts. He lives in Puerto Vallarta and works as a painter. I now understand I see my father in the attractiveness of the men I've been with. He was a man I looked up to, and any man who cared for their appearance reminded me of Dad.

After the divorce, Demian and I were on our own. Again. I sold the A-frame prefab house in Frisco and moved to Vail. I could not continue the treacherous commute over Vail Pass anymore. We found a cozy little duplex to rent in Eagle-Vail. I set up a station in the kitchen where I cut hair in between my yoga classes. *Have scissors. Will travel.*

The lifestyle in Vail attracts adventurous, athletic people. Eight or nine months of winter with dry, cold air and icy road conditions is not for everybody. As a native Coloradan, I embraced it. It reminded me of my high school days when we would travel to the mountains to spend the weekends skiing. After living in the dense brown smog of Mexico City, I appreciated the crisp, fresh air and bluebird-colored skies.

I carved out some time to ski. Some of the ski instructors invited me to ski with them. I pushed their limits in yoga class, so they did the same to me on the slopes. Thank God, I was a decent skier because skiing is not the type of sport you can master in a short period. Skiing with instructors improved my skiing dramatically. I had to keep up with everybody. I liked the pressure. They knew the mountain well, showing me their "stashes" of powder and special hidden areas for tree-skiing that called for quick, precise turns and intense concentration.

Vail was the perfect place for me to land. Many Mexicans frequent Vail and have second homes there. My friends and students from Mexico City found me, and I made an array of new friends through my teaching. I was invited to join "Chicks with Picks," a group of women who skied well and gathered in their latest Bogner outfits, complete with matching pom-pom-topped woolen hats. This was before the days of helmets. I continued to spread the word about yoga, and pretty soon, the Chicks with Picks became my students.

The only problem was Demian wasn't as happy living there. As a teenager, he missed his dad, and he didn't like the cold weather. I had a grueling schedule that demanded I be away for most of the day. After weighing the options and many hours of soul searching, I decided to send Demian to boarding school. It was a monumental decision. I was very protective of him as a result of his illness, and it was hard for me to let go. He never relapsed after he came out of intensive care, but I continued to worry about him even while he was in remission.

I was always one of those people who, when asked about doing such a thing, would answer, "There is no way I would send my child away to boarding school!" But my friend who lived close to Avon Old Farms, a boarding school in Avon, Connecticut, said she would check in on Demian. He could spend time with their family on occasion. I felt that an East Coast boarding school education was a privilege I couldn't afford.

The tuition, almost thirty thousand dollars a year, was an exorbitant amount of money for a single mom teaching yoga and cutting hair. Looking back, I can't believe I managed to pay for it, but somehow, I did.

The Yoga for Athletes Fitness Studio

In the middle of Vail, in a shopping center then called Crossroads, I opened The Yoga for Athletes Fitness Studio. People called it "the womb" because it was warm, inviting, and dark, and it was in a former subterranean bank vault.

I started out teaching the same vinyasa flow—with the Warrior variations, Crescent, Triangles, Upward and Downward Dog, and so on—that I had taught in Los Angeles and Mexico City. Teaching a number of classes and having athletically inclined students prompted me to experiment with new ways of executing the standard postures. I tested new arm positions and created novel connections between the postures. In the years following, I memorized many sequences and never planned before a class. I tuned into the room, felt the energy, and stepped aside. I let myself be a conduit between the universe and the students. It required me to have the confidence to trust the voice coming through. I focused on intuiting the needs of my students and giving them the best possible experience. I suppose it is a form of channeling. We do it when we are in that space of letting go of ego, expectations, and the background interference and moving into that pure, aligned state of being.

When I stayed in that space, I intuitively sensed where a person was experiencing pain or discomfort—and knew how to guide them. I looked at their feet and understood something subtle about them. Some people read palms; I read feet. It must sound strange, and I'm realizing just how strange as I write this, but feet speak to me. I may not remember a person's name, but I will never forget their feet and toes.

A veil, a subtle barrier, drops between the yoga teacher and student. A higher level of communication goes beyond instructional banter. The student tunes into you beyond visual posture demonstration and spoken cues. They open up and surrender to your guidance. They're seeking more than the benefits of yoga: they want you to offer them pure energy.

Standing in front of forty people who expect an enlightened experience is intimidating. Dressed minimally, with your every move under scrutiny and expectation, you feel exposed. Teaching forced me to exude confidence and believe in what I was doing.

A breath frames the beginning and end of each class. I stand silent, facing the students, ready to begin. There's a natural hush as this type of communication doesn't require words. It's far more subtle as it exists outside the realm of tangible thought, an involuntary syncing, an invitation to blithely dance with the rhythm of the breath. A gentle reminder at the apex of each pose—inhale, exhale—coaxes and cajoles the student to remain in the communal dance of the pervasive, omniscient energy.

The energy, or prana, carried by the breath works like alchemy within the body. A muscular contraction can lock onto a blocked emotion, gripping it tightly until it transforms—like ice melting into water—before finally releasing. Each posture serves a distinct purpose, and together, the sequence methodically cleanses the body, clearing the nadis (energy channels) and allowing prana to flow freely.

I have learned that a requirement of being a sound teacher is maintaining a regular personal practice. Students sense the difference between a teacher who teaches and one who lives the practice of yoga.

There's a vibration, a flow of knowledge that comes from a guide who has devoted themselves to their practice.

Distinct from the same posture in Chapter 2, it takes on an unrelated essence at this time in my life. Volcano Pose was more than a metaphor as I literally beheld with reverence another majestic mountain: the series of peaks that make up the Rocky Mountain Range running through Colorado. I was born in Boulder, at the base of this mountain range, and here I find myself once again. It feels like home, familiar. The mountains provide a perennial playground, hiking them in the summer and skiing them in the winter. Their mere presence invites ascent. After living in Mexico City, I had a renewed appreciation for the mountain air that flows through the pine trees, carrying that refreshing resinous scent. How different this time around, Upward Salute feels like a gesture of gratitude as opposed to a desperate call for help. Now I am on my way home, getting close.

The Causal Chakra, connecting us to our personal moon and the angelic realms, allowed me to develop my intuition. Teaching helped me to get out of my mind and be confident to step back and allow inspiration to come from a higher source. Rather than guiding from a pre-planned yoga sequence, I tuned into the roomful of students and allowed guidance from my higher self to take over. I felt like a conduit, a channeler. My intuition guided me and often surprised me with new information, such as a novel way to connect two postures. I sensed what was going on physically, emotionally, or mentally with a student. I felt as though I was fulfilling a portion of my life contract, doing what I came to this planet to do. This was my contribution to yoga. After everything yoga gifted me, I passed it along to others in my particular way. Through the lens of athletics and my personal filter, I was giving yoga a different language and form.

12. Bliss

Not all those who wander are lost.

—JRR Tolkien

Mountain Pose
Tadasana

Standing in this pose marks the beginning and the end of the Sun Salutation series. You connect to the earth, feel the soles of your feet on the surface and beyond, imagining and creating a deeper connection, establishing roots, and then finding strength and stability in that connection. You gaze ahead, fully focused.

Soul Star Chakra
Vyapini ~ omnipresent

The color is white. As the element of the immortal soul, it holds the information of your past lives and knows the purpose of your current embodiment. It is the link between the physical and non-physical aspects of you, residing approximately six inches above the head.

Reencountering my Greekness

Thousands of Sun Salutations lay between the earlier chapters of my life and this one that led me to another man. The relationship brought me home in unexpected ways. I met Pat in 2011 while living in Vail. Like the other men I married, meeting Pat felt serendipitous. We bonded over commonalities after discovering that he went to high school at St. Regis, where I cheered as a teen. Before long, we married.

When Pat and I purchased a home in Peloponnesus, Greece, in 2019, toggling back and forth from our homes in Vail and Los Angeles, I was called to experience a revival of my childhood memories. I saw the faces of my relatives in the community and noticed my Greek nose reflected in the women I encountered. I recognized the fortitude—and the occasional gruffness—of my personality in my daily interactions with the locals. I understood that some traits were embedded in my DNA.

When I walked through the winding corridors of the ancient town of Ermioni, inhabited since the time of Homer, the scent of food cooking transported me back to my grandmother's kitchen. Perhaps we are meant to come full circle in our lifetime. I felt comfort in revisiting the influences that had shaped who I became.

My yoga practice continued to anchor me. I flowed from one posture to the next, from inhalation to exhalation, completing a round, preparing for the next, diving forward once again. That perpetual cycle was resplendent with moments of laughter and tears, optimism and despair, love and anger, expansion and contraction. The relationship with Pat became complicated. I questioned the health of our union. I moved through time and space, gliding through thoughts and emotions, people and places, dreams and delusions—alone, and yet not.

On the Aegean Sea

I've spent many mornings paddling on the Aegean Sea. One particular morning, I felt deep gratitude for the chance to live in physical form. In what seemed to be a time of great transformation and change, the simplicity and consistency of nature soothed my soul. Tapping into it amidst the chaos of world events made it even more special.

That morning, as I pressed and pulled my paddle, propelling myself through the crystal-blue water, I noticed how the sea resembled the iris of an eye. I consciously tried to do two things: heighten my sensory perception and place myself in the role of the listener, simply observing the thoughts that rose at random. I became the witness—one of the principal practices of yogic tradition. I watched my sensations, thoughts, and reactions without judgment, attempting to be nothing more than the awareness that noticed them.

I smelled wild oregano and thyme as the breeze carried the scents from the hills to the sea. Around me, the sky shifted into shades of purple and rose, a soft palette the sun used to paint the scene. The sea and the scattered houses along the mountainside glowed with color. Birds sang their morning tunes, completing their tasks, darting from place to place, while heat climbed up my back with the rising of the sun. I tried to remain fully present, holding gratitude.

That day, I experimented with a mantra I repeated tens of thousands of times over the years: *Om Namah Shivaya*. It translates to "I honor my inner self." I asked myself what would happen if, instead of compressing it into one breath as I had always found unnatural, I inhaled with *Om*, exhaled with *Namah*, and inhaled again with *Shivaya*. Expecting a revelation, I tried it for a few minutes. I didn't slip into an altered state, but the timing felt more natural with the breath. If the mantra carried the accumulated power of those who had chanted it over hundreds of years, surely others must also have found it too wordy for a single breath.

I had been paddling for about twenty minutes when I saw what looked like Christmas lights—strands still glowing faintly, remnants of the previous night's party. I turned into the little bay where the seaside beach club, Godai, was located. Every lounge and umbrella stood ready for the weekend crowd. Mid-July marked the height of the season, when vacationers, mostly Athenians, took up summer residence near Ermioni. At 6:15 a.m., I had the place to myself. I felt like a voyeur sea goddess rising from the tides on my paddleboard, gripping a single oar, dipping it into the smooth, cool water.

After circling the village, Petrothalassa, I paddled back to the small bay where I lived. At the entrance, boulders rose on one side, resembling a giant salamander. On the other side, a massive prehistoric animal head loomed with its mouth agape. They welcomed me back as I made it to shore. It was Sunday, so the calm intensified. I couldn't resist a swim before stepping onto steady ground.

Leaving my paddleboard, I slipped into the cool embrace of the Aegean. The mineral-rich water held me effortlessly afloat, soothing and blissful, grounding me in the moment.

I often compared life to the state of mind while floating in the sea—waiting to see where the current took me. How far would I drift?

How much resistance should I apply? What stroke should I choose? Should I surrender and let myself be carried? Or return to shore and step again onto solid ground?

"The early bird catches the worm," I used to say. That day, it translated into, "The early paddler catches the calm." I marveled at the experience of being one with nature—having seen no other human being, just me alone on the sea—an enchanting opportunity to relish the beauty surrounding me.

The years dedicated to yoga, of building balance and strength, had been worth it. At seventy, I confidently set off alone across the sea with a board and paddle, watching the sunrise as one of the most precious rewards of my lifelong practice.

I did my share to keep paradise pristine. With grilling tongs and a garbage bag in hand, I collected the plastic that washed up daily on the shore. Each day brought a new assortment. That morning, it was fresh blades of grass tangled with strips of clear plastic, a block of wood with rusty nails jutting dangerously, straws, and brightly colored bottle tops. The sea expelled what she did not need, pushing it toward the sand like a child refusing food, shoving away her plate.

Another "Failed" Marriage

Nearly ten years after we married, I knew the end was coming. Thoughts kept pushing their way into my mind. *This feels like a loveless marriage. Neither of us seems happy. How can I possibly think of being single at 70? Where the hell is my soulmate?*

In the summer of 2024, Pat and I left for Greece on May 31. By mid-summer, we realized we couldn't live in the same house together. I moved back to Los Angeles.

A few weeks into that summer in Greece, before we split, I went for a massage with a mercurial, psychic intuitive. Face down on the table, she worked on my neck with immense pressure, deliberately digging deep into the bones and tissue. I drifted into a floaty, dreamlike theta state until a sensation startled me back into awareness. I turned to her and said, "It felt like you just pulled a black gob of something out of my throat." She nodded gently, offering consolation and affirmation. "Yes," was her only reply.

That night, I opened up to Pat and shared the negative thoughts about our marriage I had been suppressing for months. I felt frightened and relieved. The black gob was gone.

Not long after, back in Los Angeles, I received information about my astrological chart that helped me understand my patterns in intimate relationships. My trusted astrologer, whom I had gone to for years, told me: "Every ten to twelve years, your life completely changes—as do your partners." Listening to her felt like sitting down with Carol years before, when she knew, without my saying a word, that my parents had died when I was twelve.

Our marriage was obviously falling apart, and we weren't living in the same home, but I continued to struggle with whether to stay married to Pat. I needed this reading to understand the cycles I was repeating in relationships.

She explained that my relationships began full of hope, enthusiasm, and love, but faded and came to an end. "The karmic dance completes itself," she said. And then, somewhere, somehow, the next person appears. "Your greatest learning happens through the partners in your life." I hung on every word.

She was right. Every relationship had been laid out for me, one after the other, each helping me settle what I understood to be karmic debts—challenges or hardships carried over from past lives, offering lessons for spiritual growth. Hearing her reminded me of when, at only twenty, I visited the Vedic astrologer Chakrapani Ullal while living at the ashram in Miami. He told me I would have several partners in my life.

I felt like a seesaw, indecisively tilting from one side to the other. One day, I wanted to save my marriage, go to counseling, and try to make love with Pat again. The next day, I wanted to move on, shed the belongings that tied me down, and start fresh in a new house—maybe even in another country—with someone new. The thought of sharing my story all over again with a person who didn't know me felt daunting and overwhelming. I questioned filing for another divorce.

I saw a photo in a magazine. It was a profile of a man. I looked closely at it and thought to myself, *That is the kind of man I want.* I took a snapshot of it with my iPhone.

I wondered which of my gut feelings I could trust. My instincts changed daily, swayed by the opinions of others. The day before I snapped the photo of the guy in the magazine, I had lunch in LA with two girlfriends, women I had known for almost fifty years, part of the M7 group from our expat days in Mexico. One of them told me how difficult it was for single women living in Palm Desert, where she spent part of the year. According to her, no one asked single women out because it was a couples' world—golf, cocktails, dinners at the club, in pairs. Sure, there were occasional girls' nights or golf games, but in general, single women felt left out, especially if they were attractive. "You'd better try to work things out at this stage," she warned me. "At seventy, it isn't easy to find a man who's healthy."

The evening prior, I went to the Hollywood Bowl to see Seal in concert. He radiated pure sex appeal. He moved across the stage and into the aisles, pausing occasionally to look out at the crowd and seduce hundreds at once. I couldn't decide if it was his huge, muscular legs or the power in his movement—or perhaps that confident, penetrating stare—that made him magnetic. I hadn't been to a concert other than the Philharmonic in many years. It was new, exciting. I felt young again. I stood up, swayed to his voice, and sang along to the few lyrics I knew.

After the show, my cousin Petrula stayed the night with me. The next morning, we spoke about my tangled marriage. She offered the opposite view from my friend in Palm Desert. "I don't see you staying with Pat." She believed I should move on with a man of a different character, someone I wouldn't argue with constantly. She was sure I would find another partner; it was only a matter of time. I thought about the photo of the man in the magazine.

As I faced the end of my relationship with Pat, I felt raw and alone; tears poured down in sheets. Emotion lingered beneath the surface, waiting to spill over. Pat and I decided to divorce and sell our home in Greece.

Don't Judge My Journey

When you have been married as many times as I have, people look at you differently when you tell them you are having problems in your marriage and considering divorce. I saw their intangible thoughts take shape, floating above their heads as they listened to me speak of my unhappiness. Those thoughts read: *When is she going to realize that she is the problem?*

Out of the blue, Skip Taylor—the manager of Canned Heat and Fleetwood Mac back when I was 19 and living in LA—called me. I was astonished that he kept my phone number. Since our affair in 1976, we had spoken only once. He told me he'd had a dream the night before: we were a couple traveling through Europe. The dream was so vivid and real that he felt compelled to call me.

His voice was the same sexy, smooth, deep tone that had seduced me when we met. He spoke with perfect enunciation. His words slipped into some hidden inner space within me, stirred my emotions, and reverberated as a warm, tingling sensation throughout my body. Then came the line, one he may have said to thousands of women over the years: "Somewhere, somehow, I know we will be together." It made me melt.

Skip looked surprisingly good, considering the wild and chaotic life he had lived. Beneath the mask of his eighty-two years, I saw the young, self-assured man he once was—the high cheekbones, the electric smile. Glimpses of him surfaced in the way the corners of his mouth lifted, in the tilt of his head when he spoke, and in the way he leaned forward, as though trying to bridge the distance and reach my heart.

For a moment, I thought Skip was going to be my next one, but the universe had something else in mind. The next man hadn't appeared yet, but I sensed him—I trusted my astrological chart enough to know that when one relationship ended, the next arrived. I envisioned myself and my next person, emotionally and sensually close, touching one another constantly. That was what I yearned for: warmth, ease of physical connection, love, and tenderness.

Peter

A few months later, Demian and I were eating brunch at Saltie Girl on Sunset Boulevard in Los Angeles. It's one of my favorite neighborhood restaurants. It has a cheery atmosphere with a milky retro shade of green dominating the color palette of the tasteful décor. An urchin-shaped chandelier casts a soft glow throughout the space. An array of nautical touches and a neon sign describe a seafood eatery from another era.

Minutes into our brunch, a man entered the outdoor seating area and slid into a chair at the adjacent table, slightly in front of me. He was facing the same direction as I was. I could see his profile and thought to myself, *He looks almost exactly like the guy from the photo I took a year ago, the photo of the man that I want to be with*!

I kept glancing over at him. Something about him intrigued me. I admired how content he was sitting there by himself, occasionally looking at his phone and smiling. He ordered oysters and a mimosa. I couldn't stand it. I began searching for the photo on my phone.

Demian was watching me and asked, "Mom, what are you doing?" I explained what was going through my mind, and he sort of rolled his eyes. I found the photo and, brazenly, walked over to show it to the man. I asked him if he thought he looked like the man in the photo. He said, "Well, yeah, I can see the resemblance."

I explained I had taken the photo because I felt I wanted to be with a man like that. He laughed, and I realized it probably sounded like a pre-conceived pickup line, but that wasn't my intention. I felt compelled to talk to him. I returned to my seat, and he turned his chair to face Demian and me. His name was Peter. We chatted a bit about oysters and a few other things. When it was time to leave, I daringly asked him for his number on the premise that since he had mentioned he was new to LA and didn't have many friends yet. I could be his friend.

I think Demian was embarrassed to watch his mother acting this way. He discreetly caught my eye and mouthed the word "MOM" with a wide-eyed look on his face. In his forties, he was still my child, wondering what on earth I'd do next. Demian's cancer never returned. He chose the path of an artist, spending time in Mexico and Italy. Everyone tells him he should be a counselor. He's the person his friends rely on when they need someone to listen. Sitting at the table with him so many years after he went into remission, I didn't take for granted that he was with me the moment I met Peter. Something serendipitous was happening.

I texted Peter the next morning, casually tossing out the invitation to get together for yoga or a hike. I was comforted by his quick response, "Let's do a hike. That way we can talk." My relationship with Pat had left me feeling lonely for quite some time. Peter wanted to get to know me.

We agreed to meet the next morning at Watters Mansion in Hollywood. I had never heard of it, but it turned out to be the perfect hike—quiet, expansive views, and enough elevation to break a sweat but hold a conversation. We hiked at the same pace, and the conversation flowed sweetly and easily. There was a tangible, mutual attraction. There was an obvious, silent agreement between us to pursue another date.

I invited Peter to The Heated Room for a Flow Sculpt class with Omar Lopez. Because of the age difference (I forgot to mention he is only 52), I felt I wanted him to know I was not the normal 70-year-old in regard to physical fitness. I think he was experiencing shock and awe when he had to take a respite in child's pose while I continued blazing through the routine in the 100-degree room.

Omar reminds me of Prince, and he moves his body somewhat like Michael Jackson. With a lock of hair covering one eye and a hood covering his head, he leads class with a sexy voice that makes even counting sound erotic. The class is a combination of writhing hip movements on all fours, kicks and punches, and vinyasa flow, mixed together. The music is better than any DJ set, and everyone hangs on Omar's every breath and command. He has a well-developed lexicon that makes you want to listen and savor every word. With the heat, dim, flattering lighting, and the beat of the music, the class becomes much more than a workout. It is an experience. Peter, right next to me, was watching me, and we both enjoyed it together.

My beautiful, longtime friend, Katica, wife of Dr. Drew Francis, brains behind the established integrative medicine clinic Golden Cabinet, and mother of the famous DJ Dillon Francis, was in the class observing us. She saw a connection between me and Peter. After class, drenched in sweat, she suggested that the two of us go for a drink at Palihouse, a few blocks away. Peter and I looked at each other and both said, "Yeah, sure," not caring that salty sweat was dripping down our faces.

I never imagined I would be having this kind of sex in this época of my life!

Two months into our relationship, Peter and I spent nearly every day and night together. We didn't make love until after two weeks of sharing a bed. I believe we both wanted to savor the process, knowing sex between us was going to be special and delicious. It started with slowly cuddling and getting to know each other's bodies, leg against leg, foot caressing foot, abdomen to buttocks, arms wrapped around each other. We adjusted to the sound of each other's breath, sleeping positions, nightly rituals, and habits. It felt wondrous to observe each step, as though we were trying one another on to see if it fit—and it did.

Peter and I remain a couple in love, practicing steaming hot yoga side by side at The Center for Yoga on Larchmont in LA. It has been many years since I found myself in a crowded room with sweaty yogis, each of us trying to focus inward while inevitably sneaking glances at those around us. These days, women favor sheer shorts or leggings, styles that leave little to the imagination, and they seem more comfortable flaunting what I once would have been mortified to reveal. Back in my early yoga days, I would double-check in the mirror to make sure there wasn't the slightest hint of transparency in my bottoms.

I can't help but notice the wrinkly skin that pops into my vision when I am breathing into a posture. The straddle forward bend with hands on the ankles is the worst one because you see the crepey wrinkles on display on the arms and legs. It's not pretty, no matter how you look at it. Oh, I should be happy that at 70, I still hold my postures. Yes, I appreciate that, but it doesn't erase the vision of the crepey skin I used to associate with old women now on my body.

A few years ago, I was diagnosed with hypothyroidism, though I was asymptomatic. The low dosage of medication I'm on has not increased. Taurus rules the neck area. For that reason, I think it's a weak part of my body. I analyze physical afflictions to understand the emotional correlation. Back when I was working extended days, expending too much of my energy, I was under enormous pressure.

How can I come to terms with age? How can we reframe it? I'm still trying. The Japanese may have come the closest—seeing age as valuable, with the cracks and lines of their elders regarded with reverence and respect. A fracture in a vase is filled with gold and displayed with honor, an appreciation of imperfection. *Wabi-sabi* is the name for this way of embracing authenticity and imperfection. It looks stunning on ceramic pottery, and yes, I can even picture rugged, lined faces weathered by sun and time, proudly worn. But it's another thing to see those marks on my body and love them. Being with a younger man sharpens that struggle.

I find myself looking deeply into Peter's unlined, beautiful face—no crow's feet, no laugh lines, and he laughs often. I wonder if, when he looks at my face, he notices my jowls and the so-called "marionette lines" that frame my mouth. A few days ago, he took my photo as I was driving. He said I looked beautiful in my black turtleneck, black sunglasses, and messy, streaming hair. I liked the photo but couldn't help but see my saggy jawline. Did it really look like that?

I call Peter a highly vibrational being. He is constantly striving to be in an optimistic, positive space. He reaches for it throughout the day. Even if we wake up in the middle of the night and have a small strand of conversation about our dreams of something, he is smiling, always in a happy place. If someone says a negative comment about someone, Peter turns it into a positive. That's how he sees life.

In a world of serendipitous meetings, Peter's viewpoint is refreshing. When I met him, he reminded me of my dad. I wonder if he's Dad's soul reincarnated.

I think Peter is part of the original wave of "indigo children," the New Age concept describing highly sensitive and emotional children who are misdiagnosed with ADHD or ADD. When he was young, he had a difficult time "fitting into the box." His mind wandered, fueled by Cheerios and sugar. Teachers were not equipped to handle children like Peter, so they tried to fix them with medication. Luckily, his mother declined the idea of drugs, and today, he has the tools to navigate the world. Yoga helps him—he faithfully practices six times per week and has maintained a steady routine for over 12 years. His phone wallpaper image is a pile of indigo colored powder. He knows it. He identifies with the idea. Yoga allows him to focus and channel his creative impulses.

I haven't told him this, but I think he has the face of a Greek god. His curly black hair (salt and pepper, but mostly pepper) surrounds his bright, lit-up eyes, perfect nose, and thick lips. I especially love his lower lip, which protrudes slightly, provoking the urge for me to bite it. He is almost thirty years younger than Pat. I was craving someone who sees me like Peter does.

The palm reader was correct; I've had a very lucky and interesting life.

Extremes in My Life

If you ask me to describe my life until now, I would say it is characterized by extreme swings of misfortune to fortune.

I lost both of my parents just before my twelfth birthday.

I applied for Medicaid when I couldn't afford to pay for my son's chemotherapy treatments.

I worked full-time as a single mom, barely making ends meet on a yoga salary.

I lived in an eight-bedroom house in Greece with a beachfront facing a secluded private cove on the Aegean.

I have lived frugally in ashrams for months at a time, following a regimented schedule of meditation and chanting.

I have been a socialite in NYC, part of the ultra-rarified circle, attending charity, art, opera, ballet, and museum parties and events.

I have been genuinely in love and utterly alone.

I have been confident and self-assured, teaching yoga to thousands of people. I have been anxious and afraid to make simple decisions.

100,000 Sun Salutations Later

Salutations to you, dear Sun, I thank you for the warmth and light you have graciously showered on me every day of my life. In honoring you, I have received in return the gifts of good health and discipline, enabling me to exist in my fullest expression. I feel gratitude for the yoga teachers and students who supported me along the way. I ask myself, "What would have happened to me if I hadn't had yoga to keep me away from the temptation of drugs available to me during the wild and crazy '70s?" I was pretty much alone in the world then, with issues of abandonment from the loss of my parents. I could have turned to marijuana and cocaine as a fast escape from my problems.

A friend used to say to me, "Argie, there's one thing you can't buy. You can't buy youth." While I can't change my age, I feel young in my bones and in my soul.

What would my body look like today if I had not practiced yoga for the last fifty years? Would I have some type of disease? Would I have lost my balance and crashed while skiing? Would I have developed some eating disorder due to the stress of having my only child receive a cancer diagnosis?

How different my life would be if not for yoga. Grateful, that is how I feel, for being lucky enough to have found something that could serve as my guiding light, my key to good health, and the strong foundation on which I could experience this glorious life.

Tadasana, or Mountain Pose, marks the return to the starting point. I'm not dead yet, but I can begin to see my full circle of life. The Sun Salutation series of postures makes a return to the starting point, which is Tadasana. I am standing, connecting to the earth, but it is different now because I contain the journey of this lifetime. I feel expanded and full, strengthened and secure, a result of all I have witnessed and experienced. My connection, my grounding roots that tunnel into the earth below me, has settled in and deepened. My lifelong spiritual scouting has expanded my sense of self far beyond my physical mind and body. A part of me resides perpetually in the higher realms of consciousness.

If the Soul Star Chakra contains our spiritual gifts and accomplishments through our lifetimes, I hope to have it added to that repository. We can deposit love and kindness we've shown to others, the languages we've learned, the skills we've mastered, and the most painful lessons we've processed. In Sanskrit, the word *sadhana* means spiritual practice—whether through meditation, yoga, chanting, or simply striving to achieve perfection in all we do, in pursuit of our fullest potential. I have a sense that these are the things that make it into our Soul Star Chakra, perhaps to be tapped into and put to use the next time around.

The Present

The "present" as in now, the seventh decade of my life, and "present" as a gift, arriving healthy and happy after living such a full life. Where is the honor of coming this far, having lived 25,500 days? How is it that some societies are fully aware of the value and others are not? Where is the potentially rich exchange between generations? How can I possibly become invisible in this society? My presence contains the traces of millions of emotions that have surged through my body, thoughts that have spun out from my mind and taken residence in the layers of my body, lingering for mere seconds or settling in to repeat themselves for years. I hold the imprints of thousands of handshakes, hugs, and kisses, not to mention a rich buffet of sexual encounters.

If people take the time to listen to me, they hear the depth of lived research behind my ideas and opinions. There is a golden treasure, an infinite galaxy of words I have heard and read, gleaned from conversations with diverse people: an indigenous artist from Oaxaca, a tour guide in the caves of Dunhuang, China, a colleague from my French class in Villefranche.

I've soaked up the words from a wide spectrum of books, ranging from a fairytale by Hans Christian Andersen to a Martha Stewart cookbook to Homer's *Odyssey*. These words and the intelligent product of their assimilation all reside within me. Not only the words, but the images my eyes have absorbed remain—stored in the cells of my retina like a library of still shots and cinematic reels, drawn from the places I have traveled across the planet.

What about my dreams that take me beyond this 3D reality, the fantastical scenes and surreal travels? They have expanded my mind and enriched the library of my imagination.

All of this I hold in my being. Why can't it be seen? Has my skin become too marked with spots and scars? Has my hair grown too fine and gray? Has the loss of collagen—once holding everything in place—now made me unpleasant to look at with wrinkles and sagging muscles in its wake?

Authenticity, an inner state of peace, is the highest frequency of human emotion. Gandhi said about inner peace, "Happiness is when what you think, what you say, and what you do are in harmony." At this stage of my life, without having to prove myself at work or school or within my peer group, my authenticity is taking center stage.

My prevailing focus is to maintain the highest frequency possible, to gather my past and forthcoming experiences, and alchemize them into pure wisdom. I want to cultivate an inner state of authenticity and love so I exist from that space and transmit it wherever I go, to whomever I encounter. I aspire to do yoga for the rest of my life and continue to salute the brilliant, life-giving sun. I salute you, dear reader, for taking precious time to read my journey. I hope it has touched you in a way that inspires you to look at your life and examine it through your unique lens, and that doing so guides you to a sublime state of inner peace.

Acknowledgments

Writing this book has given me the opportunity to reunite with the people who shaped my personal journey. Years later, from a distance, I can see the growth gleaned and the lessons learned, even from the most challenging relationships. The value of and reasons for these encounters have revealed themselves through the process of writing. This reflection has offered clarity and insight into why we met.

Foremost, I acknowledge my son Demian, who continues to inspire me with his strength, depth of character, and pure soul. Being his mother, I have experienced the widest spectrum of emotions—elation, hope, deep fear, and despair. Our relationship has opened my heart and allowed me to tap into a profound inner strength I never knew I had.

To my parents and the extended Greek family on my father's side, thank you for infusing my life with a sense of pride, belonging, and identity when I needed it most. To my many dance, gymnastics, and yoga teachers, thank you for teaching me to explore and train this beautiful gift that is the physical body. To my students who taught me to teach, your unique needs and expectations pushed me to seek answers in the variations and adjustments of yoga postures. Watching you respond to my words and instructions enabled me to fine-tune and hone my teaching. To my inspiring friends, with whom I have traveled, hiked, biked, and skied, thank you for sharing in life's adventures. A heartfelt thank you to Cathy Stone, a fellow yogini and friend of 50 years, who encouraged me to write my memoir.

I owe special gratitude to Jennifer Dowd, who helped me sort and organize my writing. She saw my life as a series of encounters and greetings and gave me a structure that became *Salutations* in all its nuanced meanings.

Finally, thank you to Stephanie Fee and the team at MorphLit Press who brought this book into its final physical form.

About the Author

Argie Ligeros is a pioneer of power yoga, an accomplished athlete, and a wellness entrepreneur whose five decades of practice have inspired thousands worldwide. Her journey began in 1970s Los Angeles, where, as a young woman reeling from the sudden loss of her parents, she discovered yoga—a practice that became her anchor through love, loss, motherhood, and reinvention. Her spiritual path deepened under the guidance of Baba Muktananda and was tested to its limits when her young son faced—and survived—a battle with leukemia. Drawing on the resilience forged through these trials, Argie developed her signature Yoga for Athletes Fitness System, teaching in Mexico, Los Angeles, and Vail, Colorado, where she became known for blending spiritual wisdom with elite physical training. As Founder of RG Life, Soul Fitness for the Ages, she mentors women across generations. *Salutations* is her debut memoir—a testament to courage, transformation, and the profound practice of looking inward.

We invite you to join Argie on her socials:

♪ TikTok: @therglife_

▶ YouTube: @therglife

◉ Instagram: @therglife_

⊕ Website: www.rglife.co

About RG Life

rg *life*

Soul fitness for the ages

Argie Ligeros has devoted herself to providing extraordinary learning and life-enhancing methodologies that awaken and transform the body, mind, and soul. Her mission is to create spaces where women of all ages can bond, share insights, and grow together. She bridges generations through an inclusive exchange of vitality and wisdom. Through RG Life, she continues to guide women toward greater health, resilience, and authentic self-expression. Her work is rooted in the belief that both the physical and unseen dimensions of who we are must be nurtured to flourish.

RG Life is a unifying force built on four pillars: Physical, Metaphysical, Messenger, and Collective. Its offerings include yoga and wellness retreats, mentorship programs, and workshops. Whether you are just beginning your journey into self-discovery or deepening a lifelong practice, RG Life provides the tools and experiences to elevate both individual and shared frequencies. It helps every woman step into her highest way of being—feeling timeless, empowered, and deeply connected to herself and others.

Join Argie and the community at RG Life at
www.rglife.co